Football's Secret Trade

Since 1996, Bloomberg Press has published books for financial professionals, as well as books of general interest in investing, economics, current affairs, and policy affecting investors and business people. Titles are written by well-known practitioners, BLOOMBERG NEWS® reporters and columnists, and other leading authorities and journalists. Bloomberg Press books have been translated into more than 20 languages.

For a list of available titles, please visit our website at www.wiley.com/go/bloombergpress.

Football's Secret Trade

*How the Player
Transfer Market was
Infiltrated*

Alex Duff
Tariq Panja

WILEY | **Bloomberg**
PRESS

This edition first published 2017
© 2017 Alex Duff and Tariq Panja

Registered office

John Wiley & Sons Ltd, The Atrium, Southern Gate, Chichester, West Sussex, PO19 8SQ, United
Kingdom

For details of our global editorial offices, for customer services and for information about how to apply
for permission to reuse the copyright material in this book please see our website at www.wiley.com.

A catalogue record for this book is available from the Library of Congress.

A catalogue record for this book is available from the British Library.

ISBN 978-1-119-14542-4 (hardcover) ISBN 978-1-119-14545-5 (ebk)
ISBN 978-1-119-14544-8 (ebk)

10 9 8 7 6 5 4 3 2 1

Cover design: Wiley
Cover image: © efks/iStockphoto

Set in 12/16pt BemboStd by Thomson Digital, Noida, India
Printed in Great Britain by TJ International Ltd, Padstow, Cornwall, UK

Contents

Prologue

This book began with a riddle. We wanted to know why a company based in a redbrick house in the English town of Rochdale was lending £2 million to two-time European champion FC Porto to sign a striker. The company listed its address as 35 Princess Street, a scruffy part of town neighbouring abandoned buildings with bricked-up windows, an advice centre for the homeless and a builder's yard. CCTV cameras pointed at the front door.

It was 2010 and the Portuguese club had recently reached the last 16 of Europe's Champions League with a squad that included Radamel Falcão, Givanildo Vieira de Sousa – better known by his nickname of Hulk – and Nicolás Otamendi. Over the next few years these three players, from Colombia, Brazil and Argentina, would subsequently fetch transfer fees totalling more than €150 million and play at some of Europe's most illustrious stadiums, including Manchester United's Old Trafford and Manchester City's Etihad Stadium, a dozen or so miles away from that ordinary Rochdale house.

As the new season got underway, Porto used the £2 million loan to help finance the signing of a striker to provide cover for Falcão and Hulk. Walter da Silva, who had been raised by his mother in a Brazilian slum, was very much an unproven talent, even if he had made his debut in Brazil's Under-20 national team a year earlier.

A second company, based in London's Chancery Lane, provided another €2 million to help finance the €6 million signing. Porto's published accounts showed that this company had acquired 25% of the transfer rights of the striker. That meant it would take a quarter of any fee the striker fetched if Porto traded him to another team before his five-year contract expired.

If Da Silva went on to became as sought-after as Falcão, Hulk and Otamendi, it could turn into a lucrative investment. Although it took us three years of digging to find out who the owners of both companies were, it was clear from the start what they were doing: seeking financial returns from the football player transfer market.

Transfer fees have been part of the game since 1890, when they were introduced by the English Football Association to compensate smaller teams for losing their best players to larger clubs. Back then, there was already fierce competition among English clubs for the best talent and the manager of Preston North End, then one of the leading teams, tempted amateur players from the Scottish dockyards with money and jobs such as running a pub.

Transfer fees took longer to catch on in Italy, Spain and Germany, but were later adopted worldwide by the sport's world ruling body, the Fédération Internationale de Football Association (FIFA). FIFA regulates the thousands of cross-border transfers that take place each year.

Over the last 20 years, the international transfer market has mushroomed sevenfold in size, into a €4 billion-a-year business. The boom has been fuelled by a steady increase in income from broadcasters and an influx of billionaire owners into the game, such as Russian oligarch Roman Abramovich and Abu Dhabi's Sheikh Mansour bin Zayed Al Nahyan, who own Chelsea and Manchester City, respectively.

It was also underpinned by something else: clubs perpetually engage in panic buying of players. In 2014, Ebru Köksal, a former Morgan Stanley banker who was general secretary of Turkish club Galatasaray, explained to a room full of football financiers in Zurich: "When the Galatasaray president has a stadium full of people chanting for him to resign, he goes to the boardroom and says: sign three players." Even if, she added, the finance director says we can't afford to do that. "I'm not proud to say that for the last 10 years we've been carrying negative cash flows."

Across the game's European heartland a similar theme played out. In a study of 44 teams that year, S&P Capital IQ deemed every single one – including 20-time English champion Manchester United – below investment grade (sometimes known as "junk" grade). That's because they were ploughing most of their revenue into transfer fees and player wages in an effort to appease impatient supporters, win trophies and collect more prize money and sponsorships.

Today, the player transfer merry-go-round consumes the interest of the sports sections of tabloid newspapers and football websites, as supporters hungrily consume speculation about which player might fortify their team. The frenzy reaches a climax in Europe on August 31st and January 31st, when sleep-deprived lawyers and agents criss-cross the continent on planes trying to finalize deals before the midnight trading deadline in Europe, where most money is spent. Occasionally, they carry suitcases of cash to help ensure deals go through.

Only 10% of the 13,500 international transfers in 2014 fetched a fee, but for a few hundred elite players the fees are enormous and can top $100 million. The top end of the market is so exclusive that FIFA's former transfer market compliance chief Mark Goddard described it as "like a yacht club". There is nothing quite like it in any other sport or industry, although you could say there are some similarities with the sale of thoroughbred racehorses for millions of pounds at auction houses where Arab royalty are among the bidders.

To try and keep up with billionaire club owners like Abramovich and Sheikh Mansour, for whom money was no object, some Champions League teams had been getting finance from lenders whose identities were not immediately clear. In our search for the people behind Porto's transfer finance, our first stop was with the UK corporate register known as Companies House.

The companies in Rochdale and London's Chancery Lane each had a single named director. We contacted both of them, but neither returned our emails and letters. Between them they had been directors of more than 230 companies in Europe over the previous decade, making it likely that they were so-called nominee directors.

Such officials are hired, quite legally, for a few hundred pounds a year to sign off on company accounts. "You can form a company to do a deal, say one football transfer, and then get rid of it almost straight away and never put any information on public record," Richard Murphy, a tax expert based in Norfolk, England, told us.

We would find out that a series of UK companies had been used to finance football transfers of players over the last 15 years. There were many more such entities around the world: in Panama, Gibraltar, Malta, Luxembourg, Jersey and the British Virgin Islands, to name a few.

Acquiring the transfer rights of players was completely within FIFA's rules at the time we started investigating the practice. It had taken hold in the 1980s in South America, where clubs received finance in return for a share in the future transfer fees of young players. FIFA had long had a laissez-faire attitude to these arrangements, provided the financiers did not take control of the careers of players. We realized that these arrangements were becoming more common in Europe with the financial crisis that took hold in 2008 as high-street banks pared back lending to many clubs.

Aside from Porto, another team that had turned to private lenders was Atlético Madrid, which had been caught short by the credit crunch. Atlético was desperately trying to keep pace with Real Madrid and Barcelona, the world's biggest teams by revenue.

Finding information about these alternative finance deals was tricky. The transfer market is cloaked in secrecy, largely because clubs do not want their rivals to know what they are spending on fees. It's rare for fees to be disclosed, and less common still for club executives to discuss with reporters how they are financing the fees. Jochen Lösch, a German sports executive in São Paulo who helped run a fund that invested in the transfer rights of players, gave us his take on the new arrangements that were replacing traditional bank loans.

He said that they were already deeply entrenched in South America and parts of Europe. "It's a bit like reading *The Sun* newspaper" he said, referring to the UK tabloid newspaper known for celebrity gossip. "Everyone does it but nobody admits it." The investors did not want to be in the media spotlight that football brings. Lenders were also wary about their relationship with clubs entering the public domain.

Spanish high-street bank Bankia's partnership with Valencia football club was a case in point. Bankia's public relations department went on high alert in 2012 when the club teetered on the brink of insolvency while owing the lender 200 million euros. Having traded its best players for €95 million, the only major asset Valencia had left was its creaking Mestalla Stadium. Imagine the public backlash if Bankia had called in its debt and forced the club to sell its home.

Eventually, some club executives and lenders agreed to talk to us. They said that these private lending agreements were necessary during the credit crunch because banks had stepped back from football. The arrangements were a kind of financial hedge that allowed them to share the cost to sign players. In most other parts of the world it was a legitimate form of financing, and had been approved by stock-market regulators in Argentina and Portugal. The Spanish and Portuguese leagues endorsed the practice, as their teams were ravaged by financial meltdown.

A former English footballer in this business gave us a window into this secretive world. On a rainy day, he showed us into his ninth-floor modern office among Manchester's neo-Gothic spires. He introduced us to a sports science graduate. On his computer, the young man pulled up an eight-page file that focused on Luciano Narsingh, a winger who was born in Amsterdam.

Narsingh was coached at the Ajax youth academy that produced Johan Cruyff and Dennis Bergkamp. He did not make it into the first team, because weighing barely 60 kilos he was deemed too fragile. Now playing at PSV Eindhoven, he was starting to show that Ajax might have made a mistake in discarding him.

According to Smith's data, Narsingh was rated fourth of 80 wingers in the Dutch league, with a 69.9% score based on a variety of information such as the number of his passes that had led to a goal. That ranking made the grandson of Indian immigrants to Amsterdam a possible investment opportunity.

"This is fantasy football on steroids," explained the former player. "We are not trying to find the next star kicking a tennis ball around in São Paulo. We are higher up the food chain." He said that he had invested about $50 million on behalf of investors and was in discussions with a pair of quantitative analysts who have worked for Microsoft and Vodafone to come up with an algorithm to identify the players whose value was most likely to increase.

Betting on transfer fees was a potentially risky bet. The careers of young players can often come to nothing, through injury or just because they turn out not to be as good as people once thought they were. Only a fraction – typically less than 20% – of 16-year-olds in a club's youth team actually make it to the first-team squad.

For investors willing to take this risk, there were different variations on the same model. Sometimes they would buy stakes in players directly from a club. On other occasions they were passive investors who would put money into a transfer market fund like the one managed out of Manchester. A few times, wealthy individuals might even go as far as buying a small club for the purpose of speculating on the transfer market.

All these methods were legal. FIFA's regulations on the subject were distilled into two sentences in a sub-clause of the game's 39-page transfer rules. They said that the world ruling body has the right to sanction any club that allows a third party to interfere in player transfers. Otherwise, it did not have a problem with the practice: it did not publicly accuse or sanction any club for breaking the rule between 2008 and 2015.

Behind the scenes, we discovered investors who were speculating on the transfer boom, including oligarchs who had once been close to Abramovich and friends of the former Portuguese Prime Minister José Sócrates. Others included a British racehorse owner and a commodity magnate who normally traded not in athletes but in diamonds, gold and pharmaceuticals.

In South America, where the practice was most widespread, there were even people with ordinary jobs, such as waiters and taxi drivers, who had taken stakes in the careers of players.

We found investors who had profited from acquiring a stake in the future fees of star players including Cristiano Ronaldo, Neymar and James Rodriguez. Betting on that trio, we calculate, they netted a total of €15 million.

On the stairs of European ruling body UEFA's cavernous glass headquarters overlooking Lake Geneva, we told its then general secretary Gianni Infantino how companies in the UK whose ownership structure was not publicly available were being used to finance transfers. As we explained, Infantino frowned. "It should not be like this," he said. Even if the agreements were legal and there was no suggestion of any foul play, the Swiss-Italian said the source of the finance should be clear to make sure the integrity of football was not at risk.

Only a few years earlier, in 2007, a scandal shook the Premier League when an offshore company controlled by oligarchs engineered control over the careers of Argentine players Carlos Tevez and Javier Mascherano when they joined West Ham. The fallout took months to clear up and led to a ban on investors acquiring the transfer rights of players in the English championship.

Infantino went looking for more information about the companies bankrolling the booming transfer market during the financial crisis. He told UEFA president Michel Platini, who said he was horrified to learn that so many footballers in Europe were being used as a type of financial product, often without their knowledge.

The former English footballer in Manchester, who now ran an investment fund, told us that clubs were merely raising money against their assets, like other businesses. The career of players was not affected, he said.

Infantino's enquiries gathered pace like a "snowball", he later told us, growing as the size of the industry emerged. By 2013, investors owned stakes in the transfer rights of 1,100 players in Europe worth $1.5 billion, according to KPMG, a financial consultancy.

Over the next two years, Platini put pressure on FIFA president Sepp Blatter to ban the practice and on 1 May 2015, it was prohibited worldwide. This book tries to piece together the 30-year history of what we are calling football's secret trade, and what happened next.

Chapter 1

The Son
of Jesús

On a winter morning at Atlético Madrid's Vicente Calderón stadium, receptionists wear overcoats indoors as portable heaters struggle to provide a modicum of warmth. Madrid, which is on a plateau 600 metres above sea level and surrounded by a snow-capped mountain range, gets cold in the winter and Atlético's offices are not centrally heated.

The 55,000-seat ground is in a nondescript district south of Madrid, wedged between a six-lane ring road and a brewery. When Atlético is playing at home in the depths of winter, fans sitting in the uncovered stands are exposed to the chill wind and rain.

Atlético is the antithesis of its flashier rival Real Madrid: a working-class commoner to Real's nobility. Formed by three students, Atlético became known as "Los Colchoneros", the mattress makers, in the 1940s because their red and white shirts looked like the mattress covers that were common at the time.

When the team moved to its present stadium after the Second World War, it struggled to raise enough money to complete the arena. The arena's last major refit was in 1972, in the final years of General Francisco Franco's 36-year dictatorship.

Real Madrid (which means Royal Madrid in Spanish) is based in a stadium on the city's tree-lined main boulevard, Paseo de la Castellana. It's the equivalent of Paris having a football club on the

Champs Élysées. On the club's premises you can order sushi, jamón iberico or barbecued meat in one of three restaurants.

Team president Florentino Pérez, who is chairman of Spain's biggest building company Actividades de Construcción y Servicios, has plans to build an adjoining five-star hotel with funding from the United Arab Emirates. Real started to leave its cross-town rival in the dust in the 1950s, becoming the star of Spanish football. Then, led by the Argentine forward Alfredo di Stefano, it won five straight European Cup titles.

More recently, its model of hiring star players like David Beckham has drawn admiring write-ups in Harvard University studies that have described it as using the same model as Hollywood studios to create revenue.

On this January morning in 2013, a secretary ushering in visitors to the Calderón stadium blames the cold on the damp air blown from the nearby River Manzanares. Through a series of doors, deep inside the bowels of the old arena, Miguel Ángel Gil sits in a windowless office. Beneath black-and-white photographs of his father Jesús and mother María Ángeles, Atlético's chief executive officer is trying to keep the team operating amid Spain's worst economic crisis.

As Gil sits at his oak desk, Atlético has won only one league title since 1977. Its boardroom down the corridor is in a cramped wood-panelled space that looks like part of a 1970s suburban home and is filled with odd-looking cups and trophies from obscure competitions.

A few miles away, at Santiago Bernabéu stadium by the city's business district, Real Madrid's directors meet in a boardroom displaying replicas of a record nine identical, highly polished silver European Cups. The boardroom was redecorated as part of a €150 million refurbishment of the stadium. While Atlético doesn't have central heating, Real Madrid has fitted overhead heating outdoors to keep fans warm during games.

In Spain, the period following the two weeks of Christmas festivities is known as the "cuesta de enero", or the January hill. It's a difficult time for personal finance, when families have to pay credit card bills after extra spending on food and gifts at the same time as coping with a rise in bills from fuel and transport.

In 2013, this incline was becoming never ending for many families. The country was in the sixth year of an economic crisis, with an unemployment rate of 26%. Families were losing their homes because they could not pay the mortgage. Businesses were going to the wall at an alarming rate.

Atlético Madrid was also suffering. It was stuck with €120 million of tax debt, more than any other team in the world. No wonder it could not afford to redecorate its offices that dated back to the Franco era or install central heating. Atlético would have folded in another industry, or if it was a football club in another country.

In Scotland, Glasgow Rangers had recently been placed in administration after a claim by the UK tax authorities for six times less than what Atlético owed the Spanish treasury. Rangers, the record 54-time champion, had racked up an average annual loss of £13 million over the previous 11 years, trying to keep pace with arch rival Celtic.

Like Atlético, Rangers had sought to offset losses and pay down debt with prize money from the UEFA Champions League or the second-tier Europa League. The model collapsed when the UK tax authorities objected to a scheme to pay players via an offshore trust and ordered it to pay £21 million in back taxes. Rangers eventually went out of business as a result of the claim and was revived as a new company in the third division. Its former owner, Gil's counterpart, was banned for life from Scottish football.

Yet Atlético, fondly known as Atléti, received much more favourable treatment in Spain. It was part of Spain's social fabric: the hopeless but loveable member of the family.

Many people had a soft spot for the stoicism of its supporters. It's easy to be a fan of Real Madrid but being an Atlético fan, well that requires dedication. The club even counted the odd member of the establishment as fans, including the soon-to-be-king Prince Felipe and Economy Minister Luis de Guindos.

No government wanted to be responsible for making the club disappear. That could have been a monumental vote loser at the next polls. In 1995, a previous government had already got a taste of that when it relegated two other teams, Sevilla and Celta de Vigo, because of financial irregularities. When thousands of fans took to the streets to protest, the government hastily reversed its decision.

Apparently to avoid such a situation, the Treasury had struck a deal with Gil to pay the €120 million of back taxes by 2020 along with interest payments fixed at the modest annual rate of 4.5%. It looked like a remarkably cosy arrangement.

Gil, who controls 64% of Atlético, is a boyish-looking 50-year-old with a crooked nose and white flecks in his black curly hair. Lounging on his chair behind a mountain of papers and books on his grand oak desk, he wears his top shirt button undone and his tie askew like a naughty schoolboy. He shrugs when asked about the team's enormous tax debt. "Other teams have bank debt," he says. "We have tax debt." Politicians from the main parties were unsurprisingly slow to attack Atlético's tax situation, even as the government froze pensions and scrapped subsidies for new mothers.

We asked Miguel Cardenal, Spain's Secretary of State for Sport, about the tax deal with Atlético. Cardenal, who was new to the job, was the government official in charge of monitoring football club finances. He told us that it was normal for businesses to restructure tax debt. "It's not special treatment," he said.

It fell to an obscure regional party from Galicia, one of the country's least-populated regions, to take umbrage. "There is a dynamic in football that is totally irrational and it contaminates the public sector,"

Francisco Jorquera, the Galician party's parliamentary spokesman, said. "Many Spanish football clubs are technically bankrupt."

Atlético's woeful financial situation was a legacy of his late father, Jesús Gil. He was the most flamboyant club owner Spain has ever known. A construction magnate turned mayor of the upmarket seaside resort of Marbella, he rode into Madrid on a white horse and bathed in champagne when Atlético won the domestic league and cup double in 1996. It was a rare chance to cock a snook at Real Madrid and, well, he was not going to waste the opportunity. He never got another chance. Four years later Atlético was relegated to the second division for the first time in 65 years.

In a show of loyalty, the number of season-ticket holders almost doubled to 40,000. But fans paid less than they had a year earlier and the club had to grapple with a dramatic plunge in television income. Gil negotiated a tax moratorium with the government for two years.

More than a decade later, in 2013, Atlético still owed €46 million in back taxes from then, another €50 million following subsequent tax reviews, plus the odd €25 million it had accumulated since then.

For all that accumulated debt, Gil had just the league and cup success in 1996 to show off. That year was becoming a more distant memory each year for fans, even if they were reminded of it every time they went to a home match.

Tagged onto the side of the Vicente Calderón Stadium there is a bar called El Doblete (The Double). It is one of those archetypal Spanish bars littered with nutshells and paper napkins on the floor and serving tortilla, café con leche and beer made at the brewery a few hundred metres away.

During Madrid's stifling hot summers, Jesús would leave half of his shirt buttons undone to reveal a gold medallion as he puffed on a fat cigar. Once, at a formal dinner with other football club executives, he boasted that his first job was working in a brothel (as the bookkeeper).

He went through as many as 25 coaches in 16 years as president. "For me, firing a coach is like having a beer," he once said. "I could kick out 20 in one year, 100 if necessary."

When Miguel Ángel Gil was a five-year-old schoolboy, his father served 18 months in prison after the roof of a restaurant in a tourism complex he built 50 miles outside Madrid collapsed in 1969, killing 58 guests. The cement hadn't been given enough time to dry. Gil and his brothers were told that their father was away in a hotel, before they were old enough to know better.

Gil avoided serving more than half of the sentence thanks to a pardon from Franco, the dictator. He resurfaced in politics, becoming mayor of Marbella on a promise to cut crime and clean up the city's sleazy image.

Jesús Gil's stint in charge of Atlético was peppered with controversy. In 1989 he called French referee Michel Vautron a "maricón" (poofter) when Atlético was eliminated from the UEFA Cup by Fiorentina. Seven years later, he thumped another club's executive outside the league headquarters.

"You are a crook," Gil told his opposite number at Compostela. "And you're a son of a bitch," came the reply. Gil's riposte was a right-hander. Separated by two of Gil's bodyguards, they exchanged insults for two minutes while they climbed the stairs to the first-floor boardroom. All the while, kickback scandals mounted in Marbella. He shrugged them off until he died of a heart attack in 2004, aged 71.

The second of four children, Miguel Ángel Gil is altogether different from his roguish father. A former veterinary student, he is shy and avoids public appearances. He escapes from the pressures of managing the club's parlous finances by rearing horses, bulls, deer, birds and boars on a 2,000-acre estate near Ávila, 70 miles outside Madrid. He has one vice in common with his father: spending on player transfers. Gil was betting that his investment in signing talent would pay off, pushing Atlético higher up the standings. In turn that would trigger more prize money, and better ticket sales and sponsor-ships. It was a high-stakes roulette game that he could not afford to lose.

This business model continued to be accepted by Spanish author-ities, but worried European ruling body UEFA that was indirectly financing Atlético through prize money from the Champions League and Europa League.

Gil's bartering to sign new players would come to a head as the end-of-summer deadline approached. On 30 August 2010, a day before the trading window shut, Gil had an €11 million bid faxed to Galatasaray for midfielder Arda Turan on a single piece of A4 paper. The Turkish club rejected the offer, proudly showing off the fax to fans as proof. However, it relented for €12 million a year later and Turan was on his way to Atlético.

The signing was typical of how Gil spent money he didn't have. Atlético's cash reserves amounted to barely 5% of its €543 million debt. For the year to July 2010, just before bidding for Turan the first time around, Atlético posted a whopping €76 million loss. It was so stretched that it was late paying more than one-third of its bills, and Gil was forced to use his country house as collateral to obtain a bank loan.

Even if it was under the cosh and languishing mid-table in La Liga, Atlético was beginning to enjoy a rare patch of success in European competition under coach Enrique "Quique" Sanchez Flores, the son of an actress and nephew of a famed flamenco artist.

The high-society coach with impeccable dress sense led Atlético to the second-tier Europa League in 2010 by beating Fulham 2-1 in the final. Hugh Grant, the English actor who supported the London team, was among the crowd watching the final in Hamburg. Grant put his head in his hands as Diego Forlan scored the winning goal with four minutes of extra time remaining. In the centre of Madrid, Atlético fans converged on the Plaza Neptuno to serenade players including striker Sergio Agüero and Forlan. It was Atlético's first continental trophy since 1962.

Agüero was soon traded to Manchester City to help service the club's debt, with half of the €36 million transfer fee going to the Spanish tax agency.

Two years later, Atlético defeated Athletic Bilbao 3-0 in the Europa League final to win the title again, this time with another up-and-coming South American striker, Radamel Falcão, leading the forward line. A pattern was beginning to emerge. Gil would take on an ace young forward from South America, let him show off his talents in Europe and then trade him to a profit on the transfer market. Falcão would move on to Monaco for a €43 million fee.

The two Europa Cup wins brought Atlético €32 million in prize money from UEFA, boosting the club's income by more than 30%. But was it fair that the club continued to spend so much money on the transfer market when teams in some of Europe's other biggest leagues in the UK and Germany, such as Liverpool and Hannover, which they had defeated on the field, had to scrupulously pay their debts on time?

The European authorities were closing in on the Spanish government's laissez-faire attitude to Atlético's tax debt. The European Commission announced that it was opening an investigation into whether Atlético was receiving state aid by deferring its already-late tax payments.

On another front, the former France playmaker Michel Platini was tightening up oversight of team finances to try and create a more level playing field in UEFA competitions. Platini had parlayed a successful playing career into becoming a football administrator and was now UEFA president. It was the two-time European footballer of the year who had handed over the Europa League trophy to Atlético Madrid's victorious players in 2010 and 2012.

Platini, who had once painted over the three Adidas stripes on his football boots, saw himself as a traditionalist. He was suspicious of the money being pumped into European leagues by billionaires like Roman Abramovich, who bought Chelsea in 2003, and Malcolm Glazer, who took control of Manchester United in 2005. When he became UEFA president Platini wrote to the leaders of the European Union's 27 member nations asking them to protect football from "the malign and ever-present" influence of money.

"Money has always been in sport, and football has had a professional component for 150 years," Platini wrote. "But money has never been the ultimate objective of football: the main purpose has always been to win trophies. For the first time, we may be entering an era in which financial profit alone will be the measure of sporting success."

Platini wanted permission from the European Union to impose specific financial restrictions on football in the region. He planned to launch what UEFA called Financial Fair Play rules that aimed to stop clubs spending more than they earned.

It took him some years to achieve that support, which he eventually found from Joaquín Almunia, the Competition Commissioner who was a fan of Athletic Bilbao, the only team in Europe that shunned the player trading market; it only fielded players born or raised in the region that surrounded the club. The Basque politician met and posed for photographs several times with Platini to show his support for UEFA's move to rein in the relentless debt-fuelled spending by clubs.

Now UEFA was warning Atlético that it was among the clubs who might have millions of euros of prize money withheld from UEFA's second-tier Europa League – the competition they had won twice in the previous three years – after apparently contravening the new regulations by falling behind with bills to other clubs or tax authorities. "They've known the rules for years now," UEFA general secretary Gianni Infantino, Platini's Swiss-Italian lieutenant, said a few months after the Frenchman had handed the trophy to Atlético captain Gabriel "Gabi" Fernandez in 2012.

Atlético fans already had a gripe with Platini. After UEFA ordered the club to play two home games 300 km from Madrid following crowd disorder in 2008, they had taken to signing "Fuck Platini" at home matches. The ban was eventually revoked, but the grudge looked like it was about to get worse.

Just as Platini was getting the ear of politicians in Brussels, another issue emerged. He had heard that businessmen were seeking profit by taking stakes in the transfer rights of footballers from Atlético and other European clubs via offshore companies. The UEFA president was appalled that the careers of players had become the subject of financial speculation. It was immoral, in his view, that shares in the market value of these young athletes were being acquired by people with no connection to the game. Not only that but this was happening in the territory he oversaw. "A player's arm is owned by one person, his leg by a fund based I don't know where and his foot by a third person," Platini would later say. "I find that outrageous."

Atlético, meanwhile, was flirting with insolvency like the Spanish banks squeezed by business loan defaults and home-owners who could not honour their mortgage payments. Gil said that he could no longer extend the club's bank overdraft. Nor, in recessionary times, could he find a sponsor for the team's shirts. Ticket sales were falling as supporters lost their jobs or had their pay cut. Spain's decade-long housing bubble had burst in 2007, shedding construction jobs and ruining Atlético's project to wipe out its debt by selling its stadium to a developer and moving to a new one.

When Gil left his office at the wheel of a black Audi Q7 to join the ring road that wrapped around the Vicente Calderón Stadium, a security guard checked the coast was clear. There was always a chance of fan backlash.

A group of supporters had taken him to court, claiming a 2003 capital increase was unlawful – a claim upheld in a ruling by Spain's Supreme Court in 2014. The group maintained that Gil wasn't the rightful owner of the club. When the club was doing well, complaints subsided. When the team faltered, the vitriol returned. That's why

Atlético's form was a more pressing issue for Gil than the tax debt and, when matches were being played, he was too nervous to watch. Instead, he drove around the M30 ring road. To keep the fans happy, Gil had to find new ways to get financing. Putting in as many as 12 hours a day in his windowless office, he worked with general manager Clemente Villaverde, a silver-haired former Atlético player with a law degree, to come up with a business plan.

They started by asking foreign banks including France's BNP Paribas and Société Générale for high-interest loans and obtaining short-term finance from an unusual bunch that included a former Soviet Union official and one of Britain's wealthiest tax exiles.

When we visited them in Gil's office, cocooned deep inside the stadium, Villaverde was uneasy with us asking questions about these relationships. They were off limits for journalists, he said. "You don't ask about those kind of things." Gil appeared more relaxed but did not answer all our questions. "We are having to look elsewhere for finance because of the situation of Spanish banks" Gil said, before confirming some details of the transactions.

He said that he did not have any obligation to disclose the deals to Atlético fans. "My only duty is to the club's other shareholders," he said. The other main shareholder was Enrique Cerezo, a film production company owner in his 60s who was more outgoing and liked to appear on TV. Gil's brothers Oscar and Severiano also held small stakes.

Gil said that Platini's notion that investors were a danger to the sport's integrity because they could interfere with the careers of players was plain wrong. He said that he retained complete control over the club and its transfer decisions.

Still, Platini and his executives, who wore smart blue blazers with the UEFA emblem on the breast pocket, felt powerless to regulate the growing secondary market of transfer rights in which money was flowing to the British Virgin Islands and other offshore havens.

We are a football governing body, not a financial services watchdog, Alasdair Bell, UEFA's blunt speaking Scottish legal director, said. We can't go to all these tax jurisdictions to examine complex financial transactions.

Bell was already assembling a group of a dozen forensic account-ants to make sure that teams were complying with the Financial Fair Play rules. He had also hired accountancy firms Deloitte and Price-waterhouseCoopers as consultants on the project, and expected some hectic months ahead. During the preseason, we may be dealing with a number of clubs that are breaking the rules, he said. And, speaking as someone who likes to have a summer holiday, July and August may be a busy time.

Bell planned to spend his summer holiday in the Scottish univer-sity town of St. Andrews, where he had a home, and in the Scottish mountains. The last thing he wanted was to monitor investors betting on the transfer market. It was a role that his counterparts at world football ruling body FIFA had been shunning since the 1980s, when the practice first took off in South America.

Chapter 2

The Chess Champion

J uan Figer's greatest asset was the brain that had helped him become a chess champion in his youth. His droopy eyelids and slouching posture would make visitors to his sound-proof sixth-floor office near São Paulo's busy Avenida Paulista think he was about to fall asleep in his leather chair, but he was more likely running the numbers on his next deal. He understood the dynamics of the football transfer market as well as anyone.

Figer, a descendant of Polish immigrants to Uruguay, had worked at Peñarol, a leading team in Montevideo, in his 20s. South American teams typically had several other sports sections that ranged from rowing to water polo, and Figer was at one point head of Peñarol's chess department.

At the age of 34 he went to join his brother, who was living in São Paulo. In 1970, he arranged for Peñarol to play a friendly match against Flamengo in the Maracanã Stadium and oversaw defender Pablo Forlán's move to join São Paulo from Peñarol for an $80,000 fee. "At the time there weren't any big financial figures, people didn't get involved to become rich," Figer would later say of South American football.

That year, Pelé was wowing football fans around the world. With their canary yellow shirts on colour television for the first time, he led Brazil to a record third World Cup title in Mexico City. A 4-1 win against Italy in the final was rounded off with a flourish. Pelé nonchalantly controlled the ball and flicked it into the path of right-back Carlos Alberto Torres, who drilled a shot past Italian goalkeeper Enrico Albertosi.

Pelé's status around the world meant he was introduced to world leaders such as Henry Kissinger and John F. Kennedy. His club, Santos, took him and his club teammates on world tours that took in Hong Kong, Dubai and Nigeria, to benefit from his star status. But back home during Brazil's military dictatorship he would find that he had little wealth and his political influence was limited. He would ask the country's leader Emilio Medici for better working conditions – players were not insured against career-ending injuries and didn't receive pensions.

Medici, a straight-backed military man, would listen politely but ultimately the appeals came to nothing; the dictatorship had other concerns. It was a tense, sometimes violent time in Brazil. Soldiers sat in on editorial meetings before the nightly news. Singers and writers were living in exile in London. Opposition members were tortured. Medici liked to have Pelé as a marketing tool for the country he ruled, but football was hardly big business.

When Figer became a leading player agent in the 1980s, as the dictatorship was on its last legs, Brazilian clubs were so poorly organized that they perennially needed cash. Flamengo, the most popular team in Rio de Janeiro, had such little foresight that they would not pay Ronaldo Luis Nazário de Lima's $2 daily cross-town bus fare to its training ground as a schoolboy. Ronaldo, who eventually made a name for himself hundreds of miles away at Cruzeiro, a club in the mining state of Minas Gerais, would go on to become the World Cup's all-time top scorer with Brazil at the 2006 World Cup.

As European stadiums were upgraded, grounds in Brazil remained basic and uninviting. There was also the growing menace of fan violence, putting off the middle class from going to matches. The famed Maracanã Stadium, the iconic concrete bowl-shaped arena in Rio de Janeiro that had hosted the 1950 World Cup final, was a case in point.

Spectators who could not be bothered to queue for the toilets urinated on the access ramps, and the ammonia in their urine was gradually eating through the concrete and eroding the steel that helped support the arena. In an effort to encourage fans to use the lavatories, the Rio authorities that managed the ageing stadium upgraded them. The new toilets were something that was overdue, a stadium engineer admitted to foreign reporters. "We haven't really wanted to make the bathrooms any more enticing," he said. "The fans have a tradition of getting really mad and smashing everything in sight if their team loses. They go to the bathrooms and rip toilets from the wall and break all the pipes."

For the biggest matches such as the heaving derby between Flamengo and Fluminense, more than 100,000 fans crammed into the stadium and the structure would shake when there was a goal. But for most other league games the Maracanã was more than half empty. As few as 5,000 fans turned up.

In São Paulo, Figer spent most of his day holed up in meetings in his sixth-floor office in the Jardins neighbourhood, a tree-lined area of calm and wealth a few blocks from the bustle and traffic of the Avenida Paulista that teems with office workers and messengers on motorbikes. He had started to look for business outside his adopted home of Brazil, as his itemized telephone bill showed when it was made public years later. He made calls to contacts from the Soviet Union to Germany and the Dutch Antilles. Among visitors to his office was Pelé, who was struggling to find his way in the hard-nosed world of football business with a venture called Pelé Sports & Marketing. A cotton signed national team shirt from "Edson", Pelé's given name, hangs in the corridor of Figer's office alongside football shirts from across the globe.

To help the cash flow of chaotic Brazilian clubs in the 1980s, Figer had come up with a new strategy: he would arrange for a group of investors to advance them money in return for a cut of the burgeoning transfer market. Figer would have the players sign nominally for Central Español and Club Atlético Rentistas, two small clubs in Uruguay, and loan them immediately to first-division Brazilian teams. If a big European swooped to sign them, the return on investment could be several times the size of the stake. Teams such as Real Madrid, AS Roma and Bayer Leverkusen were starting to compete to sign players for million-dollar fees – and had their eyes on Brazil – so it was an interesting prospect.

The chess champion and his players would take a percentage of the deals, while Central Español and Rentistas would get a fixed commission for registering the players on their books without them playing in a game. It was a clever transaction, which complied with the rule book. The deals were approved by FIFA, the Swiss-based world ruling body responsible for regulating international transfers. There was no regulation stopping Figer registering the players at a club without them playing a game there and then splitting the transfer fees between as many as five parties.

In an email, a spokesman for Figer, said he always complied with the rules of his profession. He declined to make him available for an interview for this book.

During his career Figer has earned investors a share in more than $65 million in such deals, according to public records, although that number is likely to be far higher because many of the transaction fees were not disclosed. Only clubs listed on the stock market are obliged to reveal payment details.

Half of the 37 players Figer represented in 2001 had been moved through the two minor Uruguayan clubs at some point in their career. "This has been going on for years without anybody paying much attention," Rodrigo Garcia, a sports lawyer in Madrid who has represented Figer in a lawsuit, said in 2012. Asked why FIFA had not moved to stop it, he said with a shrug, "South America is a long way away from Switzerland."

Figer arranged for the investors to receive the transfer receipts via a company called Laminco International Corporation, which was set up in the offshore jurisdiction of Panama in 1997. Wealthy Brazilians were accustomed to keeping their money abroad in dollars because of the uncertainty of the Brazilian currency, the cruzeiro, and a national economy gripped by hyperinflation at the start of the decade. In 1990, inflation topped 3,000%. The value of the assets of wealthy Brazilians could change dramatically from one day to the next unless they moved their money out of the country.

Figer portrayed himself as a broker for investors in the transfer deals. He described the operations as financial risk management for clubs in which they could offset the risk of hiring a player by sharing the costs with investment funds. Among such clubs was Real Madrid, which was going through a lean spell in the mid-1990s. For years it had been trying to add to its tally of six European Cups, all but one of which were achieved with a team led by Alfredo di Stefano in the 1950s.

Like other top European clubs at the time, Real Madrid did not yet have the big television and sponsorship contracts that they command today. It had not won the continental title for three decades. Its kit was made by Kelme, a sportswear brand based near Valencia, and its shirt sponsor was a Basque household appliance maker called Teka.

The team had ceded its commercial rights to a sports agency. The team president Lorenzo Sanz, a one-time hairdresser who had grown rich from a property boom, was seeking to have another swing at the holy grail of the European Cup and started to spend on the transfer market.

A few months after hiring left-back Roberto Carlos from Inter Milan, he was offered the chance to add another promising Brazilian defender who, at age 22, was a year younger than his compatriot. Real Madrid, which ran up trading losses most years, could not afford the $6 million that Portuguesa, in São Paulo, was asking for Zé Roberto, but Figer arranged for Sanz to pay 25% of the fee and for investors to acquire the remaining 75% through one of the two Uruguayan clubs he moved players through, Central Español. Zé Roberto, a skinny livewire, did not hold down a place in Real Madrid's team coached by Fabio Capello and less than a year later he returned to Brazil.

However, the investors made a profit a few months later when he moved to Bayer Leverkusen for $14 million. Figer would celebrate each successful money-spinning deal by puffing on a Cuban cigar or strolling across the road to a restaurant for red wine and barbecued steak.

Figer avoided the limelight as much as possible. He drove a Vauxhall Opel Omega saloon with blacked-out windows and was so rarely seen in public that when the German news magazine *Spiegel* tried to get a picture of him for a story, they had to catch him by surprise in the underground car park of his office. As the camera flashed, his stunned face made him look like a rabbit caught in the glare of a car headlight.

By now, Pelé had accepted the post of Sports Minister from President Fernando Hernando Cardoso, who had stabilized the roll-ercoaster economy by replacing the cruzeiro with the real and pegging it to the dollar. In 1994, Pelé returned to Brasília with its numbered roads, office blocks and bureaucrats, a quarter of a century after hobnobbing there with Medici, the military dictator. One of his objectives under the third president of the democratic era was to give footballers more employment rights, something he had failed to do in his prime as a player.

In its final years the dictatorship had approved a law that aimed to stimulate the training of a new generation of world-beating stars. The so-called "Lei do Passe", or transfer law, gave Brazilian clubs the right to sign a contract tying a footballer to them for 10 years, until they were aged 32. The legislation gave teams more power than ever over the careers of athletes. A footballer could be fined 40% of his salary for refusing to tour abroad for 70 days of the year and could only move teams if he received permission from his employer. In Pelé's words, Brazilian footballers were treated "little better than slaves".

At the same time, Pelé attacked clubs for the slap-dash way they handled finance. "Brazilian clubs are disorganized and often deeply in debt because no one tracks their finances," Pelé said in an interview in his new office in Brasília. "When those at the top aren't taken to task, you get the mess we have now."

As Pelé tried to introduce reforms he ran into a roadblock. Eurico Miranda, the president of Rio's Vasco da Gama and a member of parliament, was among the opponents to change. He dismissed the government's plan to make clubs more commercially orientated even as, in Europe, Manchester United had started selling shares to the public. Brazilian football, the sometimes breath-taking performances of the national team, was more art than business. "Brazil isn't Europe or the U.S. when it comes to sports," Miranda said. "Here football is the highest passion. If we become companies our football wouldn't be the world's best."

There was something else that was getting in the way of Pelé's pursuit of change. Brazilian clubs were beginning to benefit from rising transfer fees. They did not want players to leave on a free transfer when they were in their prime. After failing to win enough parliamentary support for a plan to allow all players to unilaterally break their contracts at age 24, Pelé backpedalled to make it age 30. "Resistance to this type of change in Brazil is enormous," he said.

Pelé finally got through a new transfer law in 1998 that was named after him, but it was so decaffeinated from what he had originally intended that he said it barely merited his name.

And so the transfer boom continued, with Figer as the go-to man in Brazil. He cultivated contacts in Europe by sending gifts and Christmas cards. He was on first-name terms with FIFA's Brazilian president João Havelange and Joseph "Sepp" Blatter, who became FIFA general secretary in 1981.

When Figer learnt that Vasco da Gama had not paid the $1 million fee to bring back midfielder Ramon Hubner to Brazil from Bayer Leverkusen in 1996, the agent arranged for the transaction to take place two days later as a good turn to the Bundesliga team which had signed his client Zé Roberto.

As his network of contacts grew, Figer set up a European base in the same road as Madrid's Santiago Bernabéu Stadium. He also opened one in Tokyo, a popular destination for ageing Brazilian players such as 1982 World Cup star Zico. When the Internet was in its infancy in the 1990s, he had a website with photographs and profiles of players he represented. For young Brazilian players, Figer was their conduit to riches.

Footballers eyed the riches of European football hungrily. More than half of players in Brazil earned only the minimum monthly wage of 120 reais, which was then about $115. They were often desperate for financial support at the start of their career; they would sign contracts with anyone from waiters to taxi drivers who were looking for a piece of the booming transfer market.

These small-time investors used a similar finance model to Figer. They would give the player as little as $20,000 to pay for his football boots and travel expenses, or even a washing machine for his family. "People that should never have been in football were in football," Eduardo Uram, the owner of agency Brazil Soccer which represents 120 players, said. "Sometimes a guy would come to me and say I own

100 per cent of this player. I would say to him: what are you, a football club?"

Still, clubs were often willing to accommodate the waiter or the taxi driver in the deal as well as selling off tranches of the player's future transfer rights itself to, say, an investment fund. Brazilian footballer contracts had so many interested parties that they could run to 50 pages or more.

One middle-class parent in Rio de Janeiro was trying to help poor teenagers navigate this chaos to European football. José João, who went only by his two given names, had set up a football school by the beach in the neighbourhood of Flamengo almost by accident while having a kickabout with his three sons in 1988. The comfortable district was made up of palm tree-lined streets, art deco apartment blocks staffed by doormen and kiosks overflowing with magazines and newspapers for the well-off locals who could afford to buy them.

By the following year, José João had 37 students, some of them travelling on rickety buses from shantytowns perched on Rio's hills and shacks in the poor lowlands of the Baixada Fluminense. José João gave the young players access to half-decent dirt pitches, leather balls and structured games that they could not find where they lived.

Some of these teenagers were the peers of Ronaldo, the future World Cup winner who was brought up in the suburb of Bento Ribeiro and could not train with Flamengo's youth team on the wealthier south side of town because he could not afford the $2 bus fare.

José João, who abhorred how teenagers were sold or spat out by Brazilian teams, waived the fees for the children. As he supervised three five-a-side games across the road from the faded elegance of the five-star Hotel Gloria on a humid afternoon in 1999, the white-haired pensioner said he was not interested in profiting from football. He had enough to live on. "I have a small house just over there," he said, gesturing to a quiet street beyond him. "I don't want the money."

He was more concerned, he said, about the wellbeing of the children at his academy, which he called "Nova Safra" (New Crop). "I have to protect them," he said. "They don't have any idea about life. I help them learn to walk. To learn to walk they have to have a strong godfather and that's me."

José João fought with local authorities to earn the right to build artificial-turf pitches by the beach and hassled the Brazilian football federation to help fund his school. He wrote to the federation based nearby in downtown Rio asking for support. He didn't get a response, he said.

But the academy, which met only at the weekend so that children did not miss out on their education, survived with handouts from European clubs, including sets of balls and uniform. José João had an arrangement with Dutch club Feyenoord to tip them off about young players, and it would bring them to the Netherlands with their family for a trial to see if they could adapt to life in the freezing-cold port city of Rotterdam.

One of these youngsters, Leonardo Santiago, who was brought up in a slum, went for his first trial at age 11 and signed a $7,500-a-month contract at 15. Seven more players from José João's school went to play in Spain, Portugal and Italy.

It was not only offshore companies in Panama that were starting to take a cut from the boom in transfer fees. Among other beneficiaries was Parmalat, the Italian dairy company. In 1992, after taking over its local first-division team Parma and sponsoring Bernie Ecclestone's Brabham Formula One team, it turned its attention to South America.

Parmalat wanted to use Brazilian football to market its brand of milk and snacks. It struck a deal to take over the management of Palmeiras, a club in São Paulo founded by Italian immigrants. Using its know-how from Italian football, the partnership worked well and helped Parmalat make a rapid entry into Brazil. Sales rose 30% in the first year of the deal and climbed steadily over the next seven years.

The club's transfer dealings, which were overseen by Parmalat executives, provided an extra bonus. Palmeiras signed Rivaldo and Roberto Carlos to Palmeiras and cashed in by trading them to Deportivo La Coruna and Inter Milan, turning investments of a few hundred thousand dollars into millions of dollars. This tidy profit would evaporate three years later, sucked into an accounting black hole in Italy where Parmalat's parent company revealed that a $4.9 billion bank account didn't exist.

The dairy company had shown that Brazilian football had potential and Dallas-based buyout firm Hicks, Muse, Tate and Furst followed by entering Brazilian football in 1999. Its partners included Tom Hicks, who would go on to acquire Liverpool, the British football club. The Texan firm's primary goal was to start a South American cable sports channel to rival ESPN. The idea was to lure all those middle-class football fans in Brazil who preferred to watch their team in an armchair rather than in the country's basic and sometimes dangerous stadiums.

As part of a $400 million bet on the so-called Pan-American Sports Network, the Americans signed deals to manage leading first-division clubs Corinthians and Cruzeiro. The executives from the land of the National Football League and National Basketball Association, which were commercial juggernauts, would try and disprove Miranda's theory that you should not treat Brazilian football as a business. It didn't work.

One problem was that the Globo media network run by the Marinho family controlled the television market in Brazil with a mixture of soap operas, carnival parades, football and Formula One. Globo put up strong resistance to the American firm's pay-television station by buying up football rights for its free-to-air channels.

While there was sluggish take-up of subscriptions for the American channel, the firm salvaged some of its investment by trading players to Europe.

In one agreement, the Corinthians team it was managing exchanged goalkeeper Dida to AC Milan for several million dollars. "Transfers made us excellent money," one company executive recalled. "It was probably the only part of the business that was successful."

It was only late in Pelé's six-year stint as sports minister that the transactions that Figer oversaw reached the spotlight for the first time. The spark was the World Cup final in Paris between France and Brazil in 1998.

As locals crammed into packed buses to Copacabana beach in the morning to watch the final on a big screen, many wore gear with the words "A Penta é Nossa" on t-shirts and caps. It meant that Brazil's fifth World Cup was theirs, four years after the team had taken a record fourth. The host France had home advantage but hardly the pedigree of the Brazilians. As the "cariocas" chatted about the upcoming game, news filtered through by radio that the team's star player was not in the starting 15. And then, a few minutes later, that he was back on the team sheet.

Ronaldo had suffered a convulsive fit in his room at a country house where the team was staying near Paris, apparently because of nerves. His roommate Roberto Carlos sprinted up the carpeted corridor banging on all the other doors to raise the alarm. When another player, Edmundo, came running he saw Ronaldo foaming at the mouth.

When the fit subsided, Ronaldo fell asleep and doctors discussed whether to tell him what had happened in case it made him worried and ruined his performance in the match. In the end, they told him everything and Ronaldo went to a clinic for tests. French doctors said there was nothing wrong with him and the decision to omit him was quickly reversed.

In the final, however, he was a shadow of his normal self and Brazil lost 3-0. The thousands of people who had gathered on Copacabana beach went home glumly as rain started to fall. As recriminations started in the media, there were all sorts of far-fetched conspiracy theories flying about. One was that Nike had insisted that Ronaldo play in the match under the terms of its $160 million sponsorship agreement with the Brazilian football federation. It was not true – Nike only had a say in friendly games – but it was enough to kick off a parliamentary inquiry into the national game. Ronaldo was among dozens of people called to give evidence. He shrugged off all the conspiracy theories: Brazil had had a bad day at the office and lost the final, he said.

As one of the sub-plots to the headline act, Figer appeared before parliament to explain his dealings in the transfer market. Staring out through his thick, black-rimmed glasses, he was polite and precise in his answers to lawmakers. Speaking under oath, he made sure to praise his adopted homeland and answer questions politely. He carefully explained how each transaction through Uruguay worked. They could be complex. He said 25% of his client Warley Silva dos Santos's rights were owned by investors via Club Atlético Rentistas, 25% by his former club Atlético Paranaense in Brazil and 50% by the club he played for, Udinese of Italy. "A complicated operation, no?" Jurandil Juarez, an economist and federal deputy from the remote northeast state of Amapá, said to Figer. "A human being's value divided up into pieces."

Figer told the lawmakers he had not invented the practice but that it had started in Italy. In the 1960s, Raimondo Lanza du Trabia, president of the team Città di Palermo, owned the transfer rights of an Argentine player Enrique Andres Martegani himself. Transfer fees at the time were still relatively small and the practice did not catch on in Europe for several decades.

While he was polite during questioning, the former chess champion was vague about who the investors in Panama-based Laminco International Corporation actually were. He said he didn't have direct contact with the investment fund, although he gave its partners opinions about players. The Brazilian senate committee, led by Communist Party lawmaker Aldo Rebelo, concluded that Figer's arrangements bordered on illegality and were doing "serious damage" to the Brazilian treasury.

However, João Havelange, the FIFA president until 1998, and other South American football officials took a different view. They liked Figer for his efficiency and the way he was opening up the continent to bigger transfer fees from Europe. To give an example, Diego Forlán, the son of the first player Figer had brought to Brazil in 1970, would sign for Manchester United from Argentina's Independiente in an $11 million transfer – 1,350 times what his father had cost. In recognition of his work, Havelange had bestowed Figer with the honour of becoming its first registered player agent in Brazil.

Havelange's replacement, Sepp Blatter, took no action to stop the transfers Figer oversaw, even after the Brazilian parliamentary inquiry had made them public.

Another of the players Figer helped make the progression to Europe was Filipe Luís Kasmirski, who – like the agent – was a descendant of Polish immigrants to South America. Filipe Luís was raised in the southern Brazilian state of Santa Catarina and made his professional debut for Figueirense in the beach-resort town of Florianópolis at the age of 18. He quickly caught the eye as a left back and was loaned to Ajax in Amsterdam for a year. On his return to Brazil, Figer arranged for him to sign for Club Atlético Rentistas before sending him on loan to Real Madrid's second team. He eventually moved to Deportivo La Coruna for a $3 million fee, some of which ended up in the accounts of Laminco International Corporation in Panama. Filipe Luís would go on to join Atlético Madrid in 2010, when owner Miguel Ángel Gil was grappling with a worsening financial and economic crisis in Spain.

Chapter 3

The British
Tax Exile

S tuck incongruously onto the edge of Atlético Madrid's ageing Vicente Calderón Stadium, by entrance number 48 next to the M30 ring road, is a property agency called Gilmar. It's in the wistfully named Paseo de los Melancolicos. Like the stadium, it has not been refurbished for decades. The agency is part of a network of offices clustered around Madrid and Marbella, and takes its name from the surnames of Jesús Gil and his wife, María Ángeles Marin. The business is another part of the legacy to their children; while Miguel Ángel inherited Atlético, his elder brother Jesús Jr. got the property business.

When a decade-long housing bubble burst in Spain in 2007, both parts of the family business were left reeling. Jesús Jr. could not shift any houses, and Miguel Ángel could not get rid of the outdated Vicente Calderón. He had hoped to sell it to a housing developer and collect as much as €400 million to build a new stadium. With house prices falling an average of 28% in four years, developers were going out of business as they sat on brand-new properties they could not sell. There were an estimated one million empty properties across Spain. Many Spaniards had bought second homes by the beach with credit, on the assumption that property values would carry on rising.

Nevertheless, Real Madrid came out of the crash and the ensuing financial crisis smelling of roses. Real's president Florentino Pérez had

sold the club's city centre training ground for €500 million in the
sweet spot of the housing boom in 2000, and used the windfall to pay
off its debts and sign so-called "galácticos" such as Luis Figo, Zinedine
Zidane and David Beckham. In turn, the global appeal of those players
helped the club generate more money from shirt sales, sponsorship and
television income, pushing Real Madrid past Manchester United to
become the world's richest club by revenue. The signings were akin to
a Hollywood studio signing the biggest stars to generate revenue.

The arrival of Beckham, a teenage pin-up married to one of the
Spice Girls, increased shirt sales by 57% in the year after he joined.
From the moment he arrived, Beckham provided a showbusiness
edge to the team. He was tailed by paparazzi in Madrid. British
tabloids *The Sun* and the *Daily Mail* dispatched reporters to Spain
exclusively to track his moves. Before he had even played his first
game at Real's Santiago Bernabéu Stadium, he was mobbed by fans on
a pre-season tour of Japan.

When the league got underway, weekend flights from London to
Madrid filled up with British fans wanting to see him in action with
the galácticos. He might not have had the finesse on the ball of some of
his teammates, but his €25 million transfer fee was "peanuts" for the
financial return that Real Madrid got out of him, according to general
manager Jose Ángel Sanchez.

The team's income had increased fourfold to €500 million in the
last 15 years, and was now more than triple what Atlético Madrid
earned. Crucially, much of the income came from outside Spain, from
companies like Germany's Adidas and Audi, and so Real Madrid was
buffeted from the worst of the crippling economic slump at home.
There was no longer any need for Real Madrid to share transfer rights
to sign players with Panama-based investment firms like Pérez's
predecessor Loreno Sanz had done.

While Atlético Madrid's players train in a cramped, publicly
owned sports facility, Real's website boasts that its training complex

is almost three times bigger than the size of Vatican City. Built in 2005, it has a hotel and hydrotherapy centre in its grounds. Real Madrid's healthy cash flow also meant that it was able to finance the £80 million signing of Cristiano Ronaldo in 2008 with loans from Spanish banks Banco Santander and Caja Madrid. It paid the world record fee to Manchester United in a single installment.

Between 1999 and 2013, Miguel Ángel Gil's team did not win any of the 25 matches it played against Real Madrid in Spanish league and cup competitions. Not a single one in 14 years. Some teenagers had never seen Atlético Madrid beat Real Madrid. No wonder a now-famous television advertisement for Atlético showed a boy sitting in the back seat of a car asking his father: "Dad, why do we support Atlético?"

Every year, to help season ticket sales, Atlético would commission advertising agency Rushmore, owned by Martin Sorrell's WPP, to make advertisements like this, which focused on the loyalty of fans. Another ad showed Atlético's oldest season-ticket holder, 91-year-old Agustin de la Fuente Quintana, sitting in his living room in a pair of slippers. The film shows clips of a smoke-filled room, a bottle of alcohol and betting slips. "I managed to give up smoking, spirits, wine with my meals, salt, coffee, betting, cards but bloody Atléti, I can't give up," he says.

Sometimes, Atlético's fans – who self-mockingly called their own team "El Glorioso" – could only laugh at being the perennial loser to Real Madrid. Immediately after one crushing 4-1 home defeat, in which Cristiano Ronaldo scored three goals, two men in their 30s came out of the ground at door 48 and danced in the street next to the Gilmar office, chanting "Atléti, Atléti."

It looked like the situation was about to get worse. While Real Madrid managed to sign Ronaldo as the financial crisis was unfurling, Gil found that the same Spanish banks that had put up the finance for its neighbour were not willing to lend to Atlético Madrid any more. Between them, banks such as Banco Santander and BBVA held tens of billions of euros in business and home loans that were at risk of default, and the central bank was ordering them to rein in lending to all but the most solvent businesses. Real Madrid fell into that category; Atlético Madrid did not.

From his desk deep in the Vicente Calderón stadium, Gil was scrabbling around to find a way to carry on paying off the club's tax debt at the same time as fielding a competitive team. He turned to Peter Kenyon, the former Manchester United chief executive officer, for help.

Kenyon had been poached from United by Chelsea owner Roman Abramovich and was reportedly earning £3 million a year, the highest pay of any Premier League CEO. Together, they oversaw the appointment of Jose Mourinho as coach, along with a spending spree on talent. Wearing a Chelsea baseball cap over his bald head, Kenyon had put his arm around the oligarch in 2005 as they celebrated the team's first English league title in half a century. Four years later, Kenyon left the London club.

He resurfaced almost immediately to lead the international operations of Creative Artists Agency (CAA), a Beverly Hills-based company that represented dozens of actors including George Clooney and was moving into European sports. From a rented office amongst the unfashionable urban sprawl of Hammersmith in west London, Kenyon would be responsible for mapping the European sports strategy of the American showbusiness company.

CAA, which had recently signed a partnership to represent Real Madrid's Cristiano Ronaldo and Chelsea coach Jose Mourinho, issued a news release to announce its appointment of Kenyon, calling him "one of the most influential executives in global sports". It said that Kenyon had brought in £303 million of new business for United over 13 years.

In one of his first moves, Kenyon decided to set up a fund on behalf of CAA that would raise money from wealthy investors to buy the transfer rights of players from cash-strapped clubs. The showbusiness agency would receive a percentage of any profit the funds generated. While American executives had trumpeted Kenyon's appointment, they did not make any public announcement about the plan, which was marketed privately among wealthy individuals.

The venture, Quality Football Ireland, was domiciled in Ireland and Jersey for tax reasons. In company filings, Gestifute, the Portuguese management agency led by Jorge Mendes that represented Ronaldo and Mourinho, was listed as owning half the equity.

After raising more than €10 million, Kenyon and Mendes looked for clubs to do deals with. Atlético Madrid was an obvious target. Mendes and the club's owner Miguel Ángel Gil would soon become neighbours in a gated enclave in Madrid's most expensive district of Pozuelo de Alarcón. The complex of modern, open-plan buildings on the western edge of the city had been completed before Spain's property boom ended and was popular with footballers because of the privacy it afforded. Ronaldo rented a €12,000/month mansion with a swimming pool in the same secluded grounds. He could leave the enormous sliding patio doors open without any concern about paparazzi photographers or overenthusiastic fans troubling him. Other residents included Real Madrid greats Zinedine Zidane and Raul Gonzalez.

Mendes, who decorated his house with oil paintings of his two daughters and expensive Italian furniture, arranged for Kenyon and himself to have a meeting with Gil to discuss how CAA could provide a solution to Atlético's financial problems. It was not a difficult sales pitch: Gil was more desperate for cash than ever.

In March 2011, Kenyon arranged for the fund managed by CAA to pay Atlético Madrid €1.5 million in return for 40% of the transfer rights of 16-year-old youth-team player Saúl Ñiguez. The agreement was approved with a stamp by Spanish league authorities on each page and the money was transferred to Atlético's account within a week of the deal being signed.

Saúl, who went by his first name, had joined Atlético's youth team from Real Madrid and was a member of Spain's Under-17 team, which had featured some of the world's best players over recent years, including Cesc Fàbregas, David Silva and Gerard Piqué. The young midfielder was so promising that he was already training on occasion with the first team, coached by Quique Sanchez Flores. Gil said that Atlético was under no obligation to trade one of its brightest promises before his contract ran out in two years.

The terms of the 10-page contract said this too: the CAA fund was not able to exert influence over Atlético Madrid in any way. If Gil chose to retain Saúl, the fund managed by Kenyon would receive an annual interest rate of 10% for the period. That was not much more than what Spanish banks had been charging Atlético before the financial crisis blew up. Atlético needed far more than 1.5 million euros to shore up its bank balance. Making matters trickier still for Gil was that a seasoned football club lender had just quit the sport.

Investec, a bank with offices in the City of London, had for years loaned money to teams in both the Premier League and Spain's La Liga in return for promissory notes for future transfer revenue or broadcast income. This method allowed football team executives to front-load spending on player transfer fees at the start of the season, before player trading was suspended. That meant they would have a better team and more chance of finishing higher up the table and reaping financial benefits, such as qualifying for the UEFA Champions League, which pumped out €1 billion in prize money to 32 teams every year.

For most of the previous decade, Investec had forged close links with football clubs, becoming a shirt sponsor of Tottenham Hotspur, but there was increasing risk in lending to clubs after Portsmouth in 2010 became the first Premier League team to file for bankruptcy.

Under what Investec called an "idiosyncratic" rule, insolvent clubs had to pay back teams and players before financial institutions. Bank lenders and even tax authorities were further down the pecking order.

In Spain, if Atlético Madrid ran out of money, Investec would have to compete against creditors including the tax office, which it owed €120 million. The risk was too high, and in 2011 Investec got out of football, leaving Atlético looking for another financier.

But, like Kenyon, there was another powerful Briton on hand to help out: British tax exile Michael Tabor. Tabor, who was raised in the East End of London, had made his fortune by selling the 114-shop Arthur Price betting chain in 1995 to Coral. He had decided to quit rainy Britain after a particularly miserable day in Croydon, and now divided his time between a Monte Carlo apartment, where he lived with his wife Doreen, who he had been married to since 1975, and Barbados, where he was part of what the British media dubbed the "Sandy Lane" set, after the hotel of the same name they owned. Another member of the group was the billionaire currency trader Joe Lewis, another east Londoner who had acquired Tottenham Hotspur in 2001.

From his sun-splashed retreats, Tabor controlled business interests that included New York real estate and a stake in Coolmore Stud, the world's biggest thoroughbred breeder. The other members of the racing syndicate included JP McManus and John Magnier, who had built up a 29% stake in Manchester United before falling out with coach Alex Ferguson over a horse's breeding rights. They sold up to Malcolm Glazer in 2005.

Coolmore's horses had won blue-ribbon events such as the Epsom Derby and Prix de l'Arc Triomphe on the outskirts of London and Paris, and the Kentucky Derby in Louisville. The only time Tabor appeared in the public glare these days was in the refined surroundings of horse-racing paddocks. There, sometimes in a top hat and tailcoat, he would be photographed with Doreen patting one of his winning thoroughbreds.

Long ago, flush with his Coral fortune, Tabor had toyed with football club ownership when he made a bid to buy West Ham. In

1997, he was introduced to the club's owner Terry Brown by its then coach Harry Redknapp. Tabor, who had supported the club since his youth, was worried about being in the spotlight all the time. He told Redknapp so: "Harry, do I really need to sit up in that directors' box with all the fans chanting to put more money in? What do I need that for?" In the end, Tabor's offer was turned down and he went back to watching West Ham on satellite television.

When Investec pulled out of football lending, Tabor stepped in with his fortune to fill the gap. He advanced Atlético Madrid income from a broadcast deal with cable-television company Sogecable in the same way that the bank would have done. The owner of the Canal+ brand in turn paid Tabor's British Virgin Islands-based company Mousehole Limited a few months later, earning the British tax exile a handsome return on his money.

Tabor employed David McKnight, a soft-spoken Mancunian in his late 50s, and former Spanish television executive Pedro Caro to arrange the deals. After the two had agreed terms with Atlético, McKnight called in Graham Shear, a partner at law firm Berwin Leighton Paisner, who could put together a contract in as little as 24 hours. It became a well-honed routine and as well as Atlético Madrid, the group arranged similar deals with two other clubs, Deportivo La Coruna and Getafe.

The arrangements were different from those overseen by Kenyon for CAA because Tabor did not take a stake in the transfer rights of any players. His agreements were only loans that were not tied to the transfer market in any way. The deals were successful – none of the clubs defaulted – and in 2013 Tabor's associates began negotiations with Real Madrid for the entire signing fee for Gareth Bale from Tottenham. Known for his surging runs down the wing and match-winning goals, Bale was at the time a Premier League sensation. He had been voted the best player in the championship the previous season by his peers and football writers, and Tottenham did not release him without an arm wrestle over the fee. Real Madrid was locked in weeks of negotiations with Tottenham to bring yet another galáctico to the Santiago Bernabéu stadium.

They eventually reached a deal. The terms they agreed on said that Real Madrid would pay €87 million to Tottenham's HSBC bank account within 15 days or a total of €99.9 million in instalments over three years. That topped the record fee it had paid for Cristiano Ronaldo four years earlier.

Tabor's proposed loan and another financing offer by Deutsche Bank were among several which Real Madrid had on the table during negotiations. In the end, Real president Florentino Pérez said that he would draw most of the fee from the club's own cash reserves.

Michael Tabor had also taken over some of the business of Investec in English football, advancing money due to Everton, Southampton, Fulham and Reading before the start of each season in return for promissory notes from the Premier League. He even did a series of such deals with West Ham, which was by now owned by British businessmen David Gold and David Sullivan. The arrangements in the UK were through another company domiciled in the British Virgin Islands, called Vibrac Corporation.

While Investec was nervous of lending to clubs, Tabor apparently saw things differently. The Premier League's television income continued to rocket with every contract, and he was paid directly by the world's richest league. In Spain, he received his money back from television companies rather than the clubs.

Between 2011 and 2016, Tabor advanced as much as £100 million a year to clubs in Spain and England, earning himself an estimated return on investment of £60 million. Almost all the deals were smooth, although Tabor endured one hitch. Reading, a modest English club, had taken out a £10 million loan against so-called parachute payments from dropping out of the top division. But it ran into financial difficulty as Russian owner Anton Zingarevich froze his financial backing. As the club held drawn-out talks with prospective owners from Malaysia, the Football League began investigating whether Reading had allowed Vibrac to exert influence on the club's uncertain finances. Reading CEO Nigel Howe said that Vibrac merely sought to protect its financial interests and Reading was largely absolved, receiving a small £30,000 fine.

While the Vibrac name kept cropping up in the accounts of football teams, few knew who was behind it because it was based offshore. Journalists were both intrigued and frustrated by the secrecy. David Conn, a football reporter for the *Guardian* newspaper, wrote that it was "impossible" to trace the lender. Tabor, like other lenders to Premier League clubs, was entitled to keep his involvement confidential.

Fans also wanted to know more. "All I am asking for is the transparency they (the owners, Gold and Sullivan) promised when they started," Sean Whestone wrote on the fan website West Ham Til I Die. "If they haven't got the necessary liquid funds to inject into the club to help with cash flow just say so, then we will know these loans are a necessary evil with high interest."

In Spain, not even La Liga chief executive Javier Tebas was aware who was behind the loans. He shrugged his shoulders when we asked him about the Coolmore syndicate partner's involvement in financing Atlético Madrid. "It's the first I've heard of it," Tebas said. The Premier League's two-man board, Richard Scudamore and David Richards, had cleared Tabor's financing deals through Vibrac Corporation. Scudamore did not see any reason to stop team owners making agreements with offshore companies as long as he knew the source of the funds, although he monitored such arrangements more closely than ever. A few years earlier, after the most stressful period in his two decades in the job, he had changed league rules to stop investors exerting influence on player transfers.

Chapter 4

An East End Scandal

Premier League chief executive Richard Scudamore, a trim man in his 50s, was in a hurry as he took a cab to West Ham's Upton Park stadium in a scruffy part of east London in the first week of September. The club had its heyday in the 1960s, when it produced a string of talented young players. It was in the era before the transfer market took off, when commercialism had yet to take hold in the game. In 1964, the club's manager Ron Greenwood had taken the F.A. Cup trophy home on a London "tube" train wrapped in cloth after the Hammers had beaten Preston North End in the final. Two years later, three members of his team – Bobby Moore, Geoff Hurst and Martin Peters – helped England win the World Cup, snapping the dominance of Pelé and Brazil.

However, West Ham had dropped out of the Premier League in 2003, the same year that Roman Abramovich had bought Chelsea and – although it returned two years later and continued to produce talented players – it did not have the financial clout to compete with the biggest English clubs. Its latest generation of talented players – such as Rio Ferdinand, Frank Lampard and Joe Cole – had one by one left for bigger-spending clubs. The club's song, *I'm Forever Blowing Bubbles*, featuring the line "fortune's always hiding" was now more apt than ever. When Scudamore travelled there for a scheduled meeting in 2007, the club was trying to avoid relegation again.

Scudamore's car made its way down Green Street, where pie-and-mash restaurants stand next to shops selling Indian saris and samosas. Scudamore darted out of the car and strode into the club's offices to be welcomed by team managing director Paul Aldridge, who apologized for the absence of the owner, Terry Brown. Scudamore wasted no time, getting straight to the point of his visit. "These players, what's the story? How have they got here?" he snapped.

A few days earlier, in late August 2006, Carlos Tevez and Javier Mascherano had themselves arrived at West Ham. Flanking Alan Pardew, the Argentine stars held up claret and blue shirts and smiled for the media. How on earth had this struggling Premier League team managed to sign two of the world's most sought-after players? The story has its roots in South America, but was also tied to the riches that accompanied the breakup of the Soviet Union and an Israeli dealmaker called Pini Zahavi, who was never far away from football's biggest transfers.

Scudamore was already aware of wealthy individuals buying the transfer rights of players as early as 2000, a year after he took the job at the Premier League. Zahavi had told him all about it.

Zahavi was a suave and smooth-talking Israeli who had parlayed a career as a football journalist in his native Israel into a transfer broker. His first deal, while still working as a reporter, had been to take Avi Cohen to Liverpool from Maccabi Tel Aviv in 1979. After 20 years as an agent, he had turned his attention to acting as a dealmaker to help a small group of wealthy individuals, some of them from the former Soviet Union, to invest in the transfer market. He called the business Soccer Investments & Representations, or S.I.R. for short.

Zahavi's office was on a tree-lined boulevard near the Mediterranean ocean in Tel Aviv, but he spent much of his working life in five-star hotels across the globe or in his apartment in London's Marble Arch. He had learnt how this South American business model worked from his partners in Argentina: Fernando Hidalgo and Gustavo

Arribas. Together they had founded the HAZ agency, which took its name from the first letters of their surnames and used a series of companies domiciled in Gibraltar, Luxembourg and Malta to buy and sell transfer rights. The business was so successful that the trio set up their own motor-racing team in 2006, and even considered entering the USA's high-profile Nascar series before one of its drivers died in a 200 km/hr crash at the Autódromo Juan Manuel Fangio on the outskirts of Buenos Aires. The sudden and shocking death had ended their appetite to pursue the racing adventure.

Zahavi was well known in the Premier League's offices in London. At Christmas he would freight a box of oranges to Scudamore from back home. Over a cup of tea one day, Zahavi told Scudamore that he was moving into owning transfer rights. "He said I'm not an agent anymore I own players: I actually own them," Scudamore recalled. "That's the future."

In 2001, Zahavi had helped Gustavo Mascardi, the first registered FIFA agent in Argentina, earn as much as half of the $12 million transfer fee Aston Villa paid River Plate for Juan Pablo Ángel. Mascardi owned 50% of the Colombian striker's transfer rights through a company called "Siglo XXI" (Twenty-First Century). Aston Villa almost pulled out of the deal at the last minute after hearing of the unorthodox arrangement, but in the end the signing went ahead.

In the spring of 2003, Zahavi was introduced by another football agent, Jonathan Barnett, to Chelsea chief executive Trevor Birch at Les Ambassadeurs, a private club in London's Mayfair, in a move that would help him – with his contacts in the former Soviet Union – become a broker in the takeover of the then struggling club.

While Zahavi and Barnett loved the high life, fine clothes and trappings of success – like Les Ambassadeurs, which served French champagne, Belgian chocolates and Cuban cigars – Birch was a more low-key character. He had a first-class degree in accountancy from

Liverpool Polytechnic and specialized in corporate restructuring. He was an employee of Ken Bates, a gruff Londoner who had bought Chelsea for £1 in 1982.

Birch had briefed Zahavi on Chelsea's financial woes, how it could barely pay the players' salaries and how Bates wanted to sell up. The Israeli relayed the information to Abramovich. A few weeks later the Russian billionaire, dressed in jeans and accompanied by a Citibank banker and attorney from Skadden Arps law firm, came to meet Birch in one of the executive boxes overlooking the pitch at Stamford Bridge stadium. The rendezvous lasted less than an hour and ended with an outline for a deal, which was agreed on a handshake.

Chelsea's executives were stunned by how fast the Russian was moving. They did a Google search on his name but little came up. Still, he seemed to be bona fide and his advisors clearly worked for serious organizations. Three weeks later, on 1 July 2003, contracts were signed and Abramovich became the first Russian owner of a Premier League club.

Three years later, two more oligarchs who had been close to Abramovich became involved in the Premier League via a different route. Boris Berezovsky and Arkady "Badri" Patarkatsishvili took control of the transfer rights of Carlos Tevez and Javier Mascherano through a series of offshore companies and their aides arranged for the Argentines to join West Ham.

According to *The Observer* newspaper, which secured a rare interview with Zahavi that year, the Israeli acted as an advisor to West Ham in the deal just as he had done for Abramovich in his acquisition of Chelsea.

Berezovsky, a mathematician, had built his fortune after the fall of the Soviet Union by investing in Lada cars and Aeroflot planes. After surviving a car bomb that decapitated his driver during Russia's often-violent transition from communism, he masterminded Vladimir Putin's rise to power in 2000. But once the Russian president was in power, he vowed to get rid of the oligarchs for meddling in politics, forcing Berezovsky and Patarkatsishvili to flee to the UK with their fortunes.

Initially, the exiled oligarchs' link to the two Argentine players was not known. West Ham did not disclose the terms of the agreement, instead employing the clichéd patter of English football. The Hammers said that Tevez and Mascherano had "put pen to paper" on permanent contracts and all other details would remain confidential.

However, there was more going on behind the scenes. A couple of days earlier, West Ham's legal and commercial director, Scott Duxbury, had called Premier League secretary Jane Purdon to make an enquiry about the possibility of signing two players whose transfer rights were owned by offshore companies. The companies, Duxbury said, wanted the players to join West Ham free of charge should the club agree to allow them freedom to move them on. Purdon, a bespectacled lawyer from Sunderland, said the arrangement would breach league rules that forbade any third party having influence over the buying or selling of players. She advised Duxbury against the transaction.

The next day, Purdon spoke to him again and asked if there were any third parties involved in the signings. Duxbury ducked that question, according to Purdon's comments in the minutes of a Premier League hearing. "He did not say yes, he did not say no," Purdon recalled. "He merely replied that all documents required for registration had been provided. In doing so, he was in the belief that no rule had been broken."

When Scudamore personally went to West Ham to hear the club's version of events, Aldridge sought to calm him. He said there was nothing untoward. Investors were going to buy the club and therefore they were just placing these players there in anticipation of the forthcoming sale.

Scudamore, whose organization had no power to raid the club's files, went back to the Premier League's office and fumed. "When you've worked with these people for so long, when you've looked them in the eye and asked them a direct question, you get a direct answer," Scudamore said. "There's really not a lot more you can do."

If the oligarchs had been passive investors in the two players, West Ham would have complied with the rules, but it would become clear that they had complete control over the next transfer of the Argentines. According to the Premier League rules, that was not allowed. Third parties could not acquire the right to "influence" the policies or performance of teams.

The British Virgin Islands-based companies that controlled where the Argentines played next were owned by Patarkatsishvili, although Berezovsky said they were a joint venture with him under a series of gentleman's agreements they had embarked on together. They had previously held stakes in a Russian car dealership, oil company Sibneft and the *Kommersant* newspaper.

The two men now lived in exile, in mansions a 20-minute drive from each other in the Surrey commuter belt west of London. Berezovsky lived in Ascot, in an ivy-clad home with its own lake and manicured lawn. Patarkatsishvili, with his distinctive white handlebar moustache, resided in an even grander pile with chandeliers, gold fittings and ornate sculptures.

Under the deal that the two oligarchs had financed, West Ham would be a temporary home for Carlos Tevez. The club, which was founded by workers from a shipyard at the end of the 19th century, would get £2 million should he be transferred in the January transfer window three months later. After that, the compensation would fall to £100,000. West Ham would get £150,000 on the transfer of Mascherano.

Patarkatsishvili had appointed a young businessman to head up their football operation. Kia Joorabchian was raised in the UK and had previously helped his Iranian father run car dealerships in Essex and Kent. In what *Time* magazine called a "surreal" sale, the businessman in his early 30s was part of an offshore group that battled with Berezovsky for control of *Kommersant*. According to Joorabchian's version of events, he sued the oligarch over the sale before they agreed to settle out of court. "That's how I met Boris Berezovsky," he said.

Joorabchian then moved to São Paulo to manage Corinthians, one of Brazil's biggest football clubs, on behalf of the oligarchs. Patarkatsishvili's London-based Media Sports Investments (MSI) had agreed to pay $35 million to take control of the team for 10 years in return for a share of the team's profits from marketing and buying and selling players. As part of the deal, MSI would get 51% of the net profit from television revenue, sponsorships and ticket sales, and 80% of transfer fees. Joorabchian hired Tevez and Mascherano from Boca Juniors and River Plate, respectively.

Tevez's arrival thrilled Corinthian fans, who were surprised that such a big-name player had arrived on their doorstep. At $16 million he was the most expensive player ever signed by a Brazilian club. He delighted them with a never-say-die attitude that yielded 46 goals in 78 games. Tevez would celebrate each goal enthusiastically, at one point pulling a dummy from his sock and sucking on it to mark the birth of his child.

Using the wealth of the oligarchs, Corinthians went shopping in European football and added other prominent players to its squad, including Nilmar from Lyon, Gustavo Nery from Werder Bremen and Carlos Alberto Gomes de Jésus from Porto. The team swept to the Brazilian league title.

With Tevez's form pushing up his market price and triggering interest from clubs abroad, Joorabchian's job was to extract the highest possible fee for the investment fund's biggest asset. He announced that the striker would only leave Corinthians if another team paid the release clause in his contract of between £69 million and £83 million.

Even the lowest amount would have been a world record transfer fee. There was no suitor willing to hand over such an enormous sum, and so he ended up at West Ham.

The memory of the Tevez and Mascherano affair remains painful for Scudamore a decade later. "I can give you dates, I can give you times," said Scudamore, sitting at a table in his glass office that looks out at the Premier League's headquarters in a smart townhouse in London's West End. The office, with a small plaque next to the black front door, could pass for that of a law firm or accountancy practice.

In Scudamore's opinion, West Ham executives broke the rules because they were blinded by the possibility of deep-pocketed owners buying the club. "What was more tantalizing was the acquisition of the club" as opposed to the Argentine stars, Scudamore said. West Ham officials were probably "just so wrapped up in the idea of new owners, and becoming key in the new ownership structure".

In the end, neither Patarkatsishvili nor Berezovsky bought West Ham. A few weeks later, owner Terry Brown sold his majority stake in the club to a group from Iceland. Mascherano was traded to Liverpool, earning the oligarchs £18 million. A Premier League panel then issued West Ham with a record fine of £5.5 million, though it stopped short of handing down a point deduction.

To Scudamore's horror, the fallout continued. As the season reached its climax, Tevez found his form to boost West Ham's battle to avoid relegation. The Argentine scored seven goals in the last 10 games of the season, including the only one in a 1-0 win on the last day of the season at Manchester United, which kept West Ham in the top division. Tevez's goal meant that Sheffield United was relegated instead, and its coach Neil Warnock raged that Scudamore should be fired.

That single goal by Tevez made the affair "seismic rather than containable", Scudamore said. Sheffield United immediately challenged the Premier League's decision not to dock points from West Ham.

As the scandal was unfurling, Berezovsky was wrestling with dark thoughts at his home in London's commuter belt. He was feeling glum about how he had to flee Russia and had fallen out with Abramovich, who he felt had forced him into selling his oil company Sibneft below the market price. While the Chelsea owner had left Russia on a high, the former mathematician was pushed out of his country against his will. Now Abramovich, a high-school dropout, was the 15th wealthiest person in the world – worth $24 billion according to *Forbes* magazine – and had just led Chelsea to its first English league title in half a century, endearing himself to fans. Berezovsky was at 897th on the rich list, with $1.3 billion.

Berezovsky could console himself that he was on course to make more money from football. Abramovich's Chelsea had not posted a profit in each of the five years since he took charge. The London club was haemorrhaging money in the race to win trophies: in the year to June 2007 alone, Abramovich had to soak up its loss of £75 million.

Berezovzky's bet with Patarkatsishvili to buy Brazil's Corinthians was much cheaper and, despite the Premier League hullabaloo with the Tevez affair, they were now on course to turn a handsome profit by trading him for many times the $16 million they paid for him.

Still, this was not enough to lift him from his gloom. To try and claw away at some of his former ally's fortune, Berezovsky decided he would sue Abramovich over the sale of Sibneft at London's High Court. He would pursue $6 billion of his wealth.

Waiting for his moment, he carried a writ in his chauffeur-driven Maybach limousine to serve on Abramovich. One day, while shopping in Dolce & Gabbana in London's Sloane Street, Berezovsky spotted him in Hermès, another luxury store. After sneaking past Abramovich's bodyguards guarding the door of the shop, Berezovsky thrust the document in front of the startled oligarch, saying "I've got a present for you". Abramovich pulled his hands away and the paper fell to the floor. Berezovsky said the meeting was like a scene from *The Godfather* movie.

Meanwhile, the Tevez scandal rolled on until West Ham agreed to pay Sheffield United £18 million in compensation to settle the dispute almost a year later. Scudamore had already taken steps to make sure that such a case would never happen again. Seven years after chatting with Pini Zahavi over tea regarding the "future" of player trading, the Premier League boss had acted to stiffen the rules on outside investment in the transfer market. He banned third parties acquiring a stake in the transfer rights of players – even if it was a passive investment. The business model "raises too many issues over the integrity of competition and the development of young players", a Premier League spokesman said. "No-one wants to see what has happened to club football in South America repeated over here."

Patarkatsishvili's offshore companies were allowed to unwind their stakes in the rights of Tevez. They collected £9 million from loaning the striker to Manchester United for two seasons, and a further £45 million when he was transferred to Manchester City on a permanent contract in 2009.

However, the Georgian billionaire didn't live to collect his windfall. A year earlier, Patarkatsishvili had collapsed and died after dinner at his mansion in Leatherhead, aged 52. Berezovsky, who had spent the day in meetings with his friend in London, came rushing from his home when he heard the news, but police had cordoned off the mansion and would not let him in. Police would initially describe the death as suspicious, although a post mortem found that he died of a heart attack.

The Russian wept as he relayed the news of the death of his friend. "He was like my father, brother and son – all at the same time," Berezovsky told *Vanity Fair* magazine. Because their 50-50 deals were sealed on a handshake, Berezovsky now faced a fight for a share in the dead Georgian's sprawling empire. He filed a lawsuit claiming half of the $3 billion assets he left, including the company that owned Carlos Tevez's transfer rights, which had garnered £54 million.

In late 2012, Berezovsky settled out of court with Patarkatsishvili's widow Inna and her family. A few weeks earlier he had lost his lawsuit against Abramovich. On the hook for hefty legal bills from both cases, his fortune had dwindled and his status as a billionaire had vanished. The following year Berezovsky was found hanged in a bathroom at his mansion by his bodyguard. According to the insolvency division at the same High Court in London where he had duelled with Abramovich, he left debts of £300 million.

Chapter 5

The Prime Minister's Men

If Premier League chief executive Richard Scudamore was determined to keep South American football-style transfer market investors out of English football, the deepening financial crisis meant other clubs in Europe needed them more than ever. As the credit crunch spread, and Portugal requested a €78 billion bailout, the circle of investors advancing money to clubs widened to include businessmen who were close to Portuguese Prime Minister José Sócrates.

While in Brazil everyone from taxi drivers to pop stars took stakes in the future transfer rights of players, these types of investment were less common in Portugal. They were usually restricted to some of the richest and best-connected businessmen, who mixed with powerful team executives.

Among them was Paulo Lalanda de Castro, a 53-year-old Portuguese pharmaceuticals executive living abroad in a hilltop mansion a short walk from FIFA's $250 million headquarters in bucolic surroundings on a hill above Zurich. Lalanda de Castro lived in a mansion built on the side of the hill, a leafy and tranquil enclave where the Swiss elite enjoyed fine homes with views of Lake Zurich and the snow-capped Alps.

He was a board member of Octapharma, a Swiss company that manufactured potentially life-saving medicines made from human plasma for patients in intensive care. He had joined the company in 1986, just three years after it was founded. The family-owned company, which on its website described human plasma as a "precious raw material", was now turning over more than €1 billion a year. At the same time as helping save lives around the world, Octapharma was also making its directors wealthy. In 2009, Lalanda de Castro and nine other board members shared in €30 million of dividends.

The following summer, Lalanda de Castro struck a deal with FC Porto to acquire a 25% stake in the transfer rights of Brazilian striker Walter da Silva for €2 million through a company based in London's Chancery Lane, called Pearl Design Holding Ltd. By financing part of the fee paid to Brazil's Internacional of Porto Alegre, Lalanda de Castro made it possible for the Portuguese club to sign the player, who two years earlier had broken into Brazil's Under-20 team.

Walter was the youngest of six children raised by his mother, Edith, in a violent slum in the city of Recife. His 18-year-old brother was shot dead in a gang battle and he only went to school between the ages of 7 and 12. Edith managed to scrape money together to buy him football boots and get a grant for him to play in the academy of Sport, a local first-division club. It paid off: Walter scored plenty of goals, winning him a $5,000-a-month contract with Internacional in the southern city of Porto Alegre at age 17. He spent half the pay cheque to help his mother buy an apartment in one of Recife's smarter neighbourhoods.

Investors like Lalanda de Castro used UK companies for investments because they were easy to set up and, as a legacy of its colonial empire, the British Isles has tax treaties with tiny islands in the Caribbean such as Turks and Caicos and the British Virgin Islands. Setting up a company in the UK can be done online in as little as 24 hours, and costs £15. One of the few requirements is that the company has a physical address in the United Kingdom. You don't even need to say publicly what the company actually does. Lalanda de Castro hired a compatriot on the board of 80 companies in the UK and Spain to be the only public-facing official of Pearl Design Holding Ltd.

Routing transfer income offshore via London was not new in football. In 2004, Selkan Ltd, based in London's Mayfair and controlled by another company in the British Virgin Islands, helped FC Porto sign Luís Fabiano from São Paulo. When the Brazilian striker joined Sevilla for a transfer fee of €20 million the following year, it netted Selkan a return of almost €10 million.

To fund Da Silva's move to Porto, Juan Figer – the chess champion turned football agent – chipped in a €2 million loan via For Gool Co., the company that gave its address as 35 Princess Street in a scruffy part of Rochdale. The names of Pearl Design and For Gool were only made public because Porto was listed on the stock exchange and had to disclose details of all its financing deals, but the identity of Lalanda de Castro and Figer remained a mystery to all but the people involved in the transaction.

UEFA, in whose Champions League competition Porto was a regular competitor, did not know who was behind the companies. UEFA's then general secretary Gianni Infantino was exasperated. "We cannot go to the company and say please tell us who you are and what you're doing," Infantino said. "They will tell us: who are you to ask me?"

Infantino appealed to the UK government for help identifying the shareholders. While there was no suggestion of any impropriety, he wanted player trading to be more transparent. He received some support when a member of parliament brought up the issue in a debate about football governance.

Damian Collins, the MP for Folkestone, had gathered with other members of the Culture, Media and Sport Committee in a meeting room off Westminster Hall on the banks of the River Thames. The room was up the stairs from the 70 m-long Westminster Hall where Kings Charles I was tried for treason. The meeting was more of a talking shop than an urgent matter of state. The committee discussed the foreign ownership of UK football clubs such as Manchester City (owned by Sheikh Mansour bin Zayed Al Nahyan) and at times the atmosphere, following lunch, had the conviviality of a gentleman's club.

One of the pleasures of discussing sport was, said chairman John Whittingdale, another Conservative MP, discussing the topics people talk about "in living rooms, pubs and cafes". When, barely 10 minutes into the three-hour debate, another MP told how he had been a supporter of Stoke City since the age of five and requested an endorsement of the club's English owner Peter Coates, there were smiles all round. Whittingdale remarked how, before the committee meeting, they had had a sweepstake on how far into the debate he would mention Stoke City.

Collins, who gave intense interviews to media about suspect sports governance, was serious in his tone about how the "letterbox" companies were using the UK to anonymously funnel loans to Porto. "When we have a largely unregulated transfer market bringing billions of pounds into and out of the country, parliament should take an interest," Collins said. He said it was "almost impossible" to identify the companies' owners and recommended a closer look.

His comments did not gain any traction. The other members of parliament present seemed more concerned about English football clubs than FC Porto. Nor was there any official response from the government on the matter. It was hardly unusual that foreign businessmen were using UK companies anonymously. Thousands of others did the same.

Government officials defended the procedure to us by saying that they had the right to privately request the names of the shareholders. They could also, if they felt it necessary, investigate the source of the income by making enquiries with former colonies in the Caribbean.

Because there was no suggestion of any impropriety, UEFA was not permitted to peer over the wall to find out who was funding one of the teams in the Champions League. We only found out about Lalanda de Castro and Figer's loans three years later, through people involved in the deal. By the time we did find out, Lalanda de Castro was in the public spotlight for an unrelated matter after it emerged that he had arranged for former Portuguese Prime Minister José Sócrates to become an Octapharma consultant for a reputed fee of €12,000/month.

When Portuguese prosecutors began investigating Sócrates's finances, Lalanda de Castro was named as an "arguido" – the equivalent of a suspect under Portuguese law. Both men denied wrongdoing. Prosecutors gave few details of their investigations and more than 2 years later, in early 2017, prosecutors had not filed charges against either of them.

Lalanda de Castro's bet on Walter, the striker brought up in poverty, was not turning out as planned. He failed to earn a first-team place at Porto and, with his weight ballooning, was loaned out to Brazilian clubs Cruzeiro and Goiás. He became a figure of fun in his home country after his weight rose to 106 kilos and he was invited on to a popular chat show to talk in a light-hearted manner about his diet and craving for custard cream biscuits.

The remarkable thing was that he retained his instinct for goal, scoring 24 goals in as many games for Goiás, even if he did need to go on a diet. On the chat show, and down to 92 kilos while on loan at Rio's Fluminense, Walter wore a smart white shirt with the sleeves rolled up to show a tattoo of his mother Edith's name on the underside of his forearm.

In spite of his weight problems, Fluminense agreed to pay FC Porto €2 million for 25% of Walter's rights – exactly the amount Lalanda de Castro had loaned the Portuguese club. And even if there was no attractive financial return for the Octapharma executive, Lalanda de Castro at least had a clause in his deal with the Portuguese team that protected his investment. He got all of his investment money back with interest.

Two more men close to José Sócrates, the now former Prime Minister, were among the small circle of investors seeking profit from the transfer market. Carlos Santos Silva, a boyhood friend, and Rui Pedro Soares, one of his Socialist Party colleagues, had arranged transfer finance deals with Beira-Mar and other Portuguese clubs lower down the food chain than FC Porto. While the Premier League had banned this practice in England, in Portugal it was allowed and Portuguese officials even defended it as a way to help clubs who could not get bank finance.

Soares, once a youth-team player for Porto who had helped Sócrates become the Socialist Party leader, was bullish about the project in an interview with *Publico* newspaper. "On an export level," Soares said, "football must be bigger than Port wine. It's one of the viable businesses at the moment."

For Beira-Mar and other small clubs, prospects were darker than the colour of the fortified wine. Portugal had spent €600 million of public money getting 10 stadiums ready for the 2004 European Championship. The national team championship had brought tens of thousands of tourists. Television pictures showed off the country's quaint baroque architecture and golden beaches, bringing millions of euros worth of advertising. Portugal reached the final, losing 1–0 to Greece.

Now, a few years later in the dark days of the financial crisis, clubs such as Beira-Mar that had inherited these stadiums were struggling to pay the bills: the electricity charges for its $120 million arena on a highway outside the coastal town of Aveiro ran to €111,000/year. Match attendances had shrunk to 1,000 in a stadium with a capacity for 30,000. In an embarrassing low point, Beira-Mar would have to start a first-division match in 2012 with eight players after most of the squad handed in resignation letters over unpaid wages.

Portugal's former Economy Minister Augusto Mateus suggested that the empty arenas should be demolished. Maintaining a loss-making football arena with public money simply did not equate to preserving a school or hospital, Mateus said. "It's very difficult to service debt on something that doesn't create wealth or represent the public interest," he said.

For the outgoing prime minister's friends Santos Silva and Soares the numbers did add up. They saw a 34% return on their investment in the defender Yohan Tavares when, a few months later, he moved to Belgium's Standard Liège from Beira-Mar for €500,000. At the end of 2013, after acquiring the rights of a dozen players, their trading company had cash assets of €1.9 million.

■ ■ ■

Aside from nominee directors and letterbox companies, the UK offered other ways to hide the identity of shareholders from the general public. So-called bearer share companies, which could also be set up in a matter of hours, granted the holder of a share certificate the right to ownership of a corporation. Functioning like cash, the certificate did not have the name of the owner, so if it became lost or stolen there was no way to find out who it belonged to. These shares had mostly been phased out in the USA since 1982 because of their potential use in tax evasion and money laundering, but because of the mystical nature of such certificates they would remain part of Hollywood movie scripts. In the 1988 film *Die Hard* starring Bruce Willis, criminals take over an office building to steal $640 million of bearer bond certificates from a vault.

In 2002, Maurizio Delmenico, a Swiss lawyer in his late 40s, had set up a London-based bearer share company called Robi Plus Ltd that bought transfer rights. Delmenico had offered auditing and tax advice to the wealthy for two decades and, through his friendship with former Belgian footballer Luciano D'Onofrio, had become involved in the sport. D'Onofrio was the general manager of Porto for six years through to 1991, before becoming co-owner and president of Standard Liège from 1998 to 2011. The same year that D'Onofrio acquired a 25% stake in Standard Liège in a buyout with Adidas CEO Robert Louis-Dreyfus, Delmenico was elected onto the board apparently as his representative.

Two days after Christmas 2011, Delmenico acquired 10% of the rights of Porto players Eliaquim Mangala and Steven Defour on behalf of Robi Plus. That meant the company's bearer share certificate was worth at least €1.25 million. While Delmenico was the front man for the company, it was not clear who its shareholders were. Again, UEFA executives were frustrated by the UK's corporate rules. "Who is actually controlling these players?" Andrea Traverso, UEFA's head of licensing, asked. To make matters more nebulous, a Malta-based company whose shareholders were not made public acquired a 33% stake in the rights of the same footballers.

Playing out in the background was a long-running investigation in Belgium. In 2004, prosecutors began an investigation into Standard Liège's transfers dating back to the late 1990s. They formally accused D'Onofrio, Delmenico and about 20 other former directors, players and agents of crimes including tax fraud. They denied wrongdoing. The case moved at a snail's pace for more than a decade, but prosecutor Frederic Demonceau briefed us on some details. He revealed that another London-based bearer share company, Corporate Press Ltd, had been involved in Standard Liège player transfers. The company, based in the City of London and overseen by Delmenico, was set up in 2002 and voluntarily struck off in 2011.

Delmenico told us that he had set up the companies in London because he had business there. He would not say who the real owner of the companies was. Nor would D'Onofrio. When approached about Robi Plus by a reporter for France Télévisions one night in late 2012 outside his Liège apartment, the trim 57-year-old former footballer sprinted away through its narrow paved streets. The young French journalist, carrying a cardboard cutout of Mangala as a prop, gave chase for several hundred metres before giving up. By phone, D'Onofrio told the reporter "do what you have to do, but leave me in peace".

In March 2013, Robi Plus paid Lisbon-based Benfica €500,000 for the transfer rights of two 19-year-old players from Guinea-Bissau (one of the world's poorest countries, with an average annual per capita income of $600). The arrangement was a moral risk, according to Gregor Reiter, legal counsel at the European Football Agents Association, because African players are particularly vulnerable to pressure from officials to move clubs. "We have to draw the line at players becoming a commodity," Reiter said. One of the teenagers, 6-foot-1 João Mário Nunes Fernandes, was moved on by Benfica to Portugal's Atlético and second-division Desportivo de Chaves. The other, Luciano Teixeira, a 6-foot-2 defensive midfielder with a Mohican haircut, went on to play four games for France's Metz before ending up at Chaves too. By May 2015, Delmenico said he'd sold the rights of Robi Plus's players to another company. He told us he "couldn't remember" who the buyer was.

The following month, the investigation in Liège was winding up. But just as D'Onofrio was close to exhausting a second and final appeal to stop a trial, he signed a deal with prosecutors to drop the charges. The arrangement involved D'Onofrio paying more than €1 million, according to Belgium's *La Nouvelle Gazette* newspaper. His lawyer, Me Delbouille, told the newspaper that his client maintained his innocence and the deal allowed him to look to the future serenely and "not have to look into the rearview mirror all the time".

In the UK, tax avoidance – legally using often-complex corporate structures to pay less tax – had become a key political issue. Not because of the secretive football deals that were frustrating European football executives at UEFA, but after it emerged that Google, Starbucks and Amazon were using complex accounting methods to save hundreds of millions of pounds. The news caused public uproar, triggering lawmakers to take action – a reaction that the anonymous football funding had failed to ignite. It was "The Great British Tax Robbery" according to an opinion piece in the *Daily Mail* newspaper, which said that the UK was offering too many incentives for "smart" private equity owners. Company executives were hauled before parliament for questioning. Margaret Hodge, a Labour MP, told a Google executive that its accounting practices were not illegal, but immoral.

In October 2013, at a conference in London about transparency in government, Prime Minister David Cameron announced that it would do exactly what European football's UEFA had been asking: show who really owns companies. The UK government, Cameron told delegates from around the world, would require companies to publicly disclose shareholders with more than 25% of their equity. At the same time, Cameron said the UK would also ban the 1,220 bearer share companies by requiring them to convert to registered share-holders. The use of nominee directors, while not being outlawed, would also be tackled with more monitoring, Cameron said. "We need to know who really owns and controls our companies, not just who owns them legally, but who really benefits financially from their existence . . . For too long a small minority have hidden their business dealings behind a complicated web of shell companies."

In the summer of 2015, four months before its shareholders would have had to go public for the first time under the new legislation, Robi Plus's Switzerland-based director Maurizio Delmenico withdrew the company from the UK company registry.

Chapter 6

The 100-to-1
Shot

So, would the squad that Miguel Ángel Gil had assembled with the help of investors be enough to give the team a crack at the La Liga title? It seemed unlikely. Atlético Madrid would have to overcome not one but two of the most powerful clubs on the planet. Since 2005, Real Madrid and Barcelona had turned the domestic championship into a duopoly, barely losing a game all season.

Spain's recession was making the competition even more lopsided, as sponsors pulled deals with all but the biggest teams. When Korean carmaker Kia withdrew its €10 million-a-year sponsorship of the Atlético jerseys, Gil could not find a replacement. In 2012, Real Madrid finished first, Barcelona second and there was a huge 30-point gap to the third-placed team, Valencia. Atlético was another five points further back, below Málaga, in fifth place.

As Atlético slipped to a 1-0 home defeat to third-tier Albacete in the Spanish Cup three days before Christmas that season, the rumours were that coach Gregorio Manzano was on the way out. "Olé, olé, olé Cholo Simeone" fans chanted, using the nickname of Diego Simeone, one of the heroes of Atlético's team the last time it won the league in 1996. Gil hired Simeone the next day.

With the club unable to make signings in the January transfer window, Simeone worked with what he had. He instilled a new resolve in the team, turning a lacklustre squad into a determined pack who chased down every ball and relentlessly harried opponents. They played the same way he had some 15 years ago. Dressed in black, with greased-back hair that covered a growing bald patch, Simeone prowled the touchline during matches, barking orders and celebrating goals like he had scored himself. Even in his downtime he was relentless; gym goers in the upmarket suburb of Majadahonda near Atlético's training ground watched in awe as the 43-year-old went through a gruelling routine lifting weights, doing bench presses and pounding the treadmill until 10 p.m.

Behind the scenes in his windowless office at the stadium, Gil was scrabbling to raise finance to pay Atlético's bills. He raised €3 million by transferring 30% of the transfer rights of midfielder Jorge "Koke" Resurrección to the CAA fund managed by Peter Kenyon. Koke was a youth-team graduate who was soon to be called up by Spain's national team.

Gil also cobbled together €4.4 million from another fledgling hedge fund called Doyen Sports. The firm, which was based in London's Mayfair, would receive the money back plus as much as $500,000 interest from an existing kit deal Atlético had with Nike. Under the agreement, the sportswear firm would wire the money directly to Doyen's Swiss bank account from an account in the Amsterdam suburb of Hilversum.

Within weeks, Gil had raised more finance by selling 33% of the transfer rights of star striker Radamel Falcão to the same fund. The deal guaranteed Doyen at least €12 million within two years. Falcão eventually moved to Monaco for €43 million, of which Doyen received €14 million.

Gil made sure he had another striker in reserve when he let Falcão go: Diego Costa, a curly-haired tough from Brazil's poor northeast. Also in the squad that Simeone had inherited and was now whipping into shape was Diego Godin, an old-school central defender from

Uruguay who put his body on the line each game and Arda Turan, the midfielder who had arrived from Turkey.

The revitalized team's first success came in May 2013, and it could not have been sweeter. Atlético won 2-1 at Real Madrid to win the Spanish Cup for the first time since 1996, before finishing third in the league to qualify directly for Europe's Champions League for the first time in 17 years. After beating Real, Simeone said his team was giving hope to Spaniards losing their homes, their jobs and their dignity during the recession. "We are an example for the people who are suffering and for whom nothing is going right," Simeone said. "With hard work come opportunities."

The following season, Atlético won its first seven league games for the first time in its 110-year history and ended the year atop the standings. Few people believed it could last. Bloomberg Sports, a data company, using an algorithm of past performances and player transfer values, predicted before the start of the season that Atlético had a 1% chance of winning the league. The entire squad was worth less than the £80 million fee Real Madrid paid for Cristiano Ronaldo. But Atlético kept defying the odds. *El País* newspaper christened Simeone's work ethic as "cholismo", after his nickname. If Spain had an icon in the depth of the worst economic crisis in its history, it was the 44-year-old from Buenos Aires, the newspaper said.

More often than not when Gil turned on the radio or took a call while driving around the M30 ring road, his team would have just chalked up another win. Atlético players contested every ball, out-tackling their opponents. Nike erected a giant poster on the front of the Vicente Calderón stadium using one of Simeone's mantras: "Play Every Game Like It's Your Last One."

With three of the 38 games to go, Atlético looked to be heading for its first league title in 18 years. But then suddenly the players appeared to get stage fright and stumbled to a 2-0 loss at Levante and a 1-1 draw at home to Málaga. And so, on 17 May 2014, it all came down to the last day of the season. Gil's team needed a draw at Barcelona to clinch its first title since his father celebrated the 1996 triumph by riding into Madrid on a white horse and jumping into a bathtub filled with champagne.

On that final day of the season, Gil spent the warm spring morning at the team hotel, the Fairmont Rey Juan Carlos I, trying to overcome mounting nerves by discussing with colleagues who they would replace Costa and on-loan goalkeeper Thibaut Courtois with. Atlético could not hold on to the Brazilian striker because his blistering form was triggering big-money offers from England. Meanwhile, Chelsea wanted its in-form Belgian goalie to return.

At 2 p.m., four hours before kick-off, Gil and his directors headed to an uncomfortable lunch with their counterparts at Barcelona and the mayors of Spain's biggest cities. Beset by nerves, they had little appetite for the elaborate multi-course meal and political chit-chat. When the lunch was over, most of the directors of both clubs headed to Barcelona's cavernous Camp Nou stadium. The players made the trip on a bus with a police escort, edging slowly past tens of thousands of fans.

At 5.55 p.m. the teams ran out on the field in front of 98,000 fans. With Barcelona members taking up most of the allocation of tickets, there were 447 Atlético fans in one corner of the arena. They were outnumbered 220 to 1. On two sides of the stadium fans held up the burgundy and blue colours of the home team and on the other two sides they raised the red and yellow of the Catalan flag. They sang in Catalan the club anthem – *We're Barça* – whose lyrics included the lines "We've shown them all, we've shown them all, that we can never be defeated."

His heart racing, Gil slipped away from the noise. He took a taxi to Barcelona's Sants station and found a seat in a half-empty compartment on the high-speed train to Madrid. To calm his beating heart, he gulped two pills and started to watch a movie – *The Company Men*.

Starring Ben Affleck and Kevin Costner, the film is about the financial crisis and three men who are downsizing after losing their jobs. As the train picked up speed to 190 miles-per-hour through the rocky landscape around Zaragoza, dotted with lakes and pine trees, Gil managed to block out what was happening in the match. A ticket inspector asked if he wanted to know the score. "No thanks," he said.

It was not going well. Costa pulled up with a hamstring injury after 13 minutes and then, before half-time, Barcelona's Lionel Messi chested down the ball into the path of Alexis Sanchez, who fired Barcelona into a 1-0 lead. A friend called Gil to let him know.

As half-time approached, the few Atlético fans in the stadium started bracing themselves for missing out on the title on the last day of the season. But then, four minutes into the second half, Atlético's captain Godin headed into the net from a corner to make it 1-1. Television cameras picked out one Atlético fan jumping up and down on the spot and screaming deliriously.

On the train, Gil could no longer hold back his curiosity and turned on his mobile phone, clicking on a La Liga app. He saw what half of Spain already knew – Atlético was back on course for the title. He kept his eyes trained on the small screen for the next 40 minutes.

Messi had a goal disallowed but by the time the train pulled into Madrid's Atocha station at dusk, there was no further score and Atlético Madrid was league champion. Gil tried not to show his emotion as he walked calmly to the taxi rank, but he felt like punching the air as all the stress of the last few months gave way to delight.

As tradition dictated, thousands of Atlético fans gathered to celebrate in Madrid's Neptune Square, a downtown plaza which has a statue of the Greek god of the sea in the centre. The square is next to the Ritz Hotel and Prado museum, which houses a fabulous art collection worth billions of euros, including "Las Meninas", the 17th-century masterpiece by Diego Velázquez. It was an unlikely setting for Atlético's working-class fans.

Gil did not join them as his father had two decades previously. And there would be no champagne bath either. Later that night he celebrated more sensibly with the players at the Asador Donostiarra restaurant close to the Real Madrid stadium. On starched white tablecloths, they gorged themselves on jamón ibérico (Spanish cured ham), rioja wine and steak. The dinner ended in the early hours of the morning with sweets, liqueurs, drunken backslapping and embraces. Almost everyone attributed the success to Simeone. Still, Gil praised himself; he had hired the inspirational coach and picked the right players in the transfer market. "It's something I've been doing for 20 years," he said.

The season was not over. A week later, Atlético faced Real Madrid in the Champions League in Lisbon in its first elite European final since 1974 after eliminating Barcelona and Chelsea. Tens of thousands of madrileños made the 300-mile road trip to Lisbon. The city's hotels were booked up. Atlético and Real Madrid fans flocked into the 60,000-seat Estádio da Luz stadium together. Some Atlético supporters wore red and white shirts from the 1990s with "Marbella" on the front, a legacy of the Jesús Gil era. If Atlético won, it would be the club with the least financial resources since FC Porto to take the elite European title.

Atlético, skilfully maintaining possession, took a first-half lead on another Godin header. The underdog appeared to be heading to its first Champions League title, before a loss of concentration in the third minute of stoppage time allowed Sergio Ramos to equalize with a header. The roar from Real Madrid fans was deafening after 93 minutes of pent-up frustration.

Ramos's late goal felt like a kick in the gut to Simeone's men. The team collapsed in extra time. Gareth Bale made it 2-1 after pouncing when Atlético goalkeeper Thibaut Courtois parried a shot. Real Madrid substitute Marcelo ran through the exhausted defence and fired in another goal and Ronaldo made it 4-1 with a penalty kick. He tore off his shirt and posed for the cameras like the Incredible Hulk.

With his team in tatters, Simeone sprinted onto the field to confront Real Madrid's French defender Raphaël Varane, whom he accused of disrespectfully kicking the ball towards him and his colleagues. Held back by several Atlético players, Simeone received a red card. After almost tasting victory, the game ended in ignominy.

Michel Platini, a fierce opponent of the debt-laden business model Atlético has adopted, handed the silver trophy to Real Madrid captain Iker Casillas with a grin on his face. Platini, standing next to his right-hand man Gianni Infantino, patted his French compatriot Karim Benzema on the back. An hour later, journalists from around the world applauded Simeone as he arrived for a post-match news conference. "I feel bruised but not sadness," he said. "I'm proud of the extraordinary season we've had."

A few hundred metres away, Real Madrid's president Florentino Pérez – still immaculate in grey suit, monogrammed shirt and tie – congratulated his players on the team's first Champions League title since 2002. It had got through roughly $1 billion in transfer fees since then. Asked if the team would pare back spending now, Pérez's director Pedro Lopez said "that's enough" before adding a proviso, "but the summer is just starting".

Pérez and Lopez left the stadium together in the back seat of a chauffeur-driven Audi A8 estate, and would soon be plotting their next assault on club football's biggest prize.

Two months later, Real Madrid signed Colombian playmaker James Rodriguez, one of the stars of the World Cup, from Monaco for as much as $100 million. That meant Pérez has been responsible for four of the five most expensive signings in football history. The other belonged to Barcelona, which added Luis Suárez from Liverpool for about $80 million.

Meanwhile, Gil had to juggle with back taxes, interest charges and payments to transfer right investors. He traded top scorer Diego Costa to Chelsea for some $50 million to service debt, marking another payday for the Brazilian's agent Jorge Mendes, who had brought him to Madrid in flip-flops eight years earlier.

■ ■ ■

Jorge Mendes is on a 350-mile road trip. It's a summer's day and he's driving fast through the parched land of central Spain. His Porsche slides past the isolated medieval towns of Ávila and Salamanca and vast expanses of uninhabited land used for little else than the rearing of fighting bulls and the production of cured ham. For much of the deserted motorway between Madrid and Oporto, the road narrows into a dual carriageway and Mendes steps on the accelerator to weave past lumbering trucks heading in both directions. He chats to his flame-haired girlfriend, Sandra, who is in the passenger seat, about their plans for the future.

It's 2002 and Mendes, who is 36, is working hard to get himself known as a football player agent. He knows it is important to mix among the leading coaches and executives, and that is why he is racing to get home to grab some rest before catching scheduled flights to London and then Manchester to meet Manchester United manager Alex Ferguson. He will be representing Ricardo Lopez, a goalkeeper from Madrid whom Ferguson is interested in recruiting from Real Zaragoza.

Suddenly, the rhythm of the journey is interrupted: an axle clanks off a truck in front of his car and Mendes swerves to avoid the huge piece of metal and loses control. The Porsche spins into a guardrail, and the airbags open. Stunned but still conscious, Mendes takes a few moments to understand what has just happened. He checks Sandra is also okay and climbs out of the vehicle with his face bloodied. One of his first thoughts is the meeting with Ferguson. An ambulance arrives and takes the couple to hospital for a check-up. Skin has been torn from his ear but there are no serious injuries.

Mendes leaves and gets back on the road to Oporto's Francisco de Sá Carneiro airport. As the TAP airline takes off and flies over Spain's Basque country he is dabbing the raw skin of his damaged ear to stop blood dripping onto his suit. The plane lands at London and he takes a second flight to Manchester. After shaking hands with Ferguson, he takes a seat with an assortment of agents and representatives of both clubs to thrash out a deal. Mendes surreptitiously dabs at the wound, shifting his side to Ferguson so the Manchester United manager cannot see what he is doing. But Mendes is only a bit-part player in the swift negotiations and Ferguson barely notices him.

A few years earlier Mendes had been earning a living by running a video rental store in a nondescript arcade on the outskirts of the northern Portuguese town of Viana do Castelo. He also played for the local amateur team. As a sideline he would sell advertising space on hoardings at the team's tiny stadium, but before long he set himself the goal of representing more talented teammates in the world of professional football.

At the age of 27, he would make a 300-mile round trip several times a week to try and place goalkeeper Nuno Espírito Santo, across the border in Spain at Deportivo La Coruna. On arriving, he went to the offices of the club's president Augusto Lendoiro unannounced. Sometimes, Lendoiro would have time to talk at a restaurant by the stadium overlooking the Atlantic Ocean. On other occasions, Lendoiro would make his excuses and Mendes would have wasted his journey and petrol money.

When he got the chance, Mendes would mine the amiable former politician for information about the football business. At the time, Deportivo was a powerhouse in Spain and Lendoiro had signed Brazilian striker Bebeto and defender Mauro Silva to help the team take on Real Madrid and Barcelona. Lendoiro would recount tales such as how he had travelled to Brazil with pictures of the beach in La Coruna to coax Bebeto into joining his club rather than Borussia Dortmund, which was also trying to sign him. In Germany, Lendoiro told him, it always rained. Perched on the edge of northwest Spain, La Coruna was hardly sun-kissed but Bebeto settled in quickly and scored 86 goals over the next four years.

Mendes eventually persuaded Lendoiro to sign Espírito Santo from Vitoria Guimarães as a reserve keeper, and the rookie Portuguese agent had his first break. That gave him more credibility and persuaded more players to use him as their agent. Mendes still affectionately calls Lendoiro "padrino" (godfather) for giving him his first break, and the two speak regularly by phone.

One of Mendes's growing stable of clients was a 17-year-old Sporting Clube de Portugal player called Cristiano Ronaldo, whom he persuaded to join him. With the supremely talented teenager as one of his clients, Jorge Mendes did not have to go running around to meetings any more. Manchester United's Ferguson came to see him and his teenage client instead. In the Lisbon seaside suburb of Cascais in the summer of 2002, Ferguson persuaded Ronaldo to sign for United rather than Juventus, Real Madrid or Arsenal.

As Mendes became more influential, he began to take a financial interest in the transfer rights of some of the players he represented. In December 2006, a 19-year-old Brazilian stepped off a plane wearing flip-flops to be greeted by temperatures of −4°C in Madrid. Diego Costa had raw talent but had not received any coaching until the age of 15. He also had a quick temper and easily got into fights. Mendes had organized for the raw striker to come to Europe to mature. He took a 30% share in his transfer rights with Sporting Braga, which in its accounts called the arrangement an investment partnership. It was the start of Mendes's participation in the transfer rights business and a friendship with the Portuguese club's president Antonio Salvador. Over the coming years he would acquire the rights of more than half a dozen South American players in deals involving Braga.

Costa initially struggled to adapt to the colder weather in the north of Portugal and was homesick for his family and home-cooked rice, beans and barbecued meat. But Atlético saw enough talent in the raw striker and Miguel Ángel Gil agreed to sign him, acquiring 50% of his transfer rights for €1.5 million.

Both Braga and Mendes retained a share in Costa's transfer rights, and as he became accustomed to life in Spain his form improved and the agent's bet paid out for everyone involved with his $50 million move to Chelsea.

Chapter 7

The Switzerland of South America

By the time of the 2008 financial crisis, Juan Figer was in his mid-70s and winding down his career. By his own reckoning the first FIFA-authorized agent in Brazil had brokered more than 1,000 transfers in the four decades since he arrived from Uruguay as a young man. Dozens of the trades had been routed through his native country for the benefit of the shareholders of Panama-based Laminco Corporation International. The procedure had survived a parliamentary inquiry in his adopted home and was still operational, although on a smaller scale.

It was time for Figer to relax a little and reacquaint himself with his homeland, which he had left all those years ago. Now he would spend the summer months in the Uruguayan beach resort of Punta del Este while his sons Marcel and André oversaw business back in landlocked São Paulo. "I got used to the city but I miss the sea, now more than ever," he told Brazilian newspaper *O Globo*. "I was born in Montevideo, near the water."

But, while the transfer market veteran did not have the energy to jet around the world anymore and had closed his offices in Madrid and Tokyo, he could still pull off a big deal thanks to his contacts, including his old friend Jorge Nuno Pinto da Costa, who was also into his eighth decade.

Figer had known the FC Porto president for the best part of three decades. Their relationship dated back to 1986 when the agent represented Walter Casagrande, a 6-foot-3 striker who played for Brazilian club Corinthians. Casagrande, part of Brazil's 1986 World Cup squad, had fallen out with the club and Figer acquired control of his transfer rights. With his cut of this arrangement, the striker bought an apartment for himself and one for his parents on the outskirts of São Paulo. In a stopgap measure, Figer arranged for Pinto da Costa to take Casagrande on loan for six months at Porto. It was a surprise for the 23-year-old player because he wanted to follow his former Corinthians teammate Sócrates and play in Italy, then the most prestigious league in Europe.

As northern Portugal's winter closed in, Casagrande found himself alone, without his family, and miserable in a hotel. He would later admit in his authorized biography to experimenting with heroin in local bars during those dark days. By the summer he was off to Italy's Serie A to play for Ascoli after a $750,000 transfer and he and Figer were back in business.

Figer and Pinto da Costa had much to reminisce about from these days. They could also talk about FC Porto's 2-1 come-from-behind win against Bayern Munich in the 1987 European Cup final in Vienna. Rabah Madjer, an Algerian, scored the equalizer for Porto with an exquisite back heel in the 87th minute. Juary, a Brazilian forward, scored the winner three minutes later to seal Pinto da Costa's place in the folklore of his home city. Porto went on to win the Intercontinental Cup by beating Peñarol, the club Figer was still a fan of, even after almost 40 years of living in Brazil. "A man can change his wife, his political party but not his football team," Figer said.

Neither of the two elderly men was ready to retire. In 2008, Figer arranged for Givanildo Vieira de Sousa – better known as Hulk because of his impressive physique – to move through Club Atlético Rentistas to FC Porto.

Hulk who, like other Figer clients, did not actually play in a match for Rentistas had been contracted to Tokyo Verdy in Japan until a few weeks earlier. The deal earned Panama-based Laminco as much as $19 million and was perhaps the most lucrative deal Figer had pulled off for the offshore company's shareholders, whoever they were.

The following year, two Englishmen left London's rain-swept autumn to go to the same resort where Figer spent the summer. They checked in to the Conrad Punta del Este Resort & Casino hotel, which billed itself as a Las Vegas-style betting oasis with 75 card-playing tables and 500 slot machines. Malcolm Caine, a man in his 60s with thinning white hair and a slight paunch, lived in a $2 million townhouse in a leafy north London cul-de-sac in St. John's Wood. He was a racehorse owner whose friends included Jonathan Barnett, one of the UK's most prominent football agents.

Barnett, who had begun his working life in his family's casino business, had built up his client base by agreeing to represent eight members of England's Under-16 team after approaching them and their parents after a match against Germany in the English town of Chesterfield in the early 1990s. He had begun to represent Gareth Bale as a 15-year-old, eventually negotiating his move to Real Madrid. Now the Stellar Group agency he had founded with David Manasseh represented some 200 footballers. *Forbes* magazine rated Barnett as the fourth highest-earning agent in sports, pulling in $44 million a year in commissions. That put him behind only Americans Scott Boras and Tom Condon, and Ronaldo's Portuguese agent Jorge Mendes according to the magazine.

Barnett would occasionally break from his hectic work schedule to go to the races with Caine and watch their horses in action. On a May evening in 2014, they saw their four-year-old gelding Café Society come first in a seven-horse field at Windsor, west of London, for its third victory in 18 months. A few days later, they sold the horse at an auction in London to a group of Australians for £330,000.

On the trip to South America, Caine's companion was a lawyer more than a decade his junior. Graham Shear held a 5% stake in Barnett and Manasseh's Stellar Group. Shear was familiar with the world of football finances. He had helped Michael Tabor, the British bookmaker turned racehorse owner, draw up more than a dozen loan agreements with Spanish and Premier League clubs through offshore companies. Over a month in late 2009, Caine and Shear met four or five of second-division Uruguayan club Deportivo Maldonado's directors at the casino hotel.

It was spring south of the equator and the resort was quiet before the start of the summer holidays, which coincided with Christmas and New Year in this part of the world. Most of the blinds were shut in the whitewashed condominiums overlooking the beach. Although fishermen were busy each morning on their scruffy tugboats, the harbour was not yet heaving with the pristine mega yachts that would arrive in a few weeks when South America's jet set arrived.

Three miles inland from the beach strip, Deportivo Maldonado's humble stadium was of a different social standing from the holiday destination that attracted the region's high rollers. The club's offices were in a small building with fading green paint. The team's emblem, an unhappy-looking whale spouting water, was also etched on the façade. The building looked more like a primary school than a football club's headquarters. A few rows of uncovered concrete terracing served as seating for the 200 or so fans that bothered to turn up for home games.

As part of his investment in the obscure club, the British racehorse owner planned to buy the transfer rights of players from across South America, typically those in their national Under-20 teams, before trading them to European clubs. It was a variation of the so-called 'pases puente' or bridge transfers that Juan Figer had been arranging through Uruguayan clubs since the 1980s. The difference was that Caine actually owned this team. He pledged to cover the expenses of

Deportivo Maldonado's football operation. The average wage of a second-division player in Uruguay was as little as $600 a month at the time, meaning that the Englishman would have to cover an annual payroll cost of about $150,000. That was less than what Gareth Bale earned in a single week at Real Madrid.

The discussions, conducted politely in English, were productive and eight days before Christmas, contracts were signed. Caine registered a new company to control the football club. The formation of Deportivo Maldonado's holding company was made official in Montevideo.

Under Uruguayan law, the company had to have at least five directors. Caine became president and appointed his sons by his South African wife, David and Leon, as directors, along with two Uruguayan administrators. Shear became vice-president. There was no press conference or press release to mark the event. In fact, little seemed to change.

Caine's arrival was hardly noticed in this quiet backwater of South American football: Maldonado failed to win any of its first six games under its British owner, and finished the season ninth out of 13 second-division teams. But, it was making several moves in the transfer market. In one of his first deals, Caine signed Willian José da Silva, who had recently broken into Brazil's Under-20 team.

Willian José's story was typical of the rags-to-riches life of many Brazilian footballers. He was one of five children of a security guard and housewife from Porto Calvo in the northeast state of Alagoas. The small town is dominated by a whitewashed church – Our Lady of the Presentation – built by Portuguese settlers in the 17th century. The Portuguese had exported sugar and wood from the dense woodland around the town back to Europe.

The Da Silva family lived in one of the dozens of simple one-storey homes leading out to fields. As a 10-year-old child, Willian José used to earn pocket money by carting the shopping of locals at a

Saturday street market to their homes in a wheelbarrow. But he preferred to take afternoon naps in the shade of the church and told his mother, Edileusa, that he was too shy for the work.

At age 12, he got into football, a relative latecomer in Brazil. He quickly made an impression for his poise and fierce shooting, and three years later was offered a contract by Gremio Barueri, 1,200 miles away in São Paulo.

He went to Brazil's biggest metropolis with his elder brother Washington as a chaperone. Just as the brothers arrived, the team began rising up through the divisions and was soon taking on Brazil's biggest clubs, thrusting the timid boy forward into the spotlight. He excelled, scoring 15 goals in one season, and was suddenly in demand.

By now, he had his own agent, Nick Arcuri, who advised him to sign for Deportivo Maldonado. Willian José said he did not go to Uruguay to register with the club, nor had he any intention of playing there. All the paperwork was done in São Paulo, he said. He was immediately loaned to the first-division team of the same name, São Paulo, where he became an understudy to national team striker Luis Fabiano.

He initially found it difficult to adapt to the pace and pressure of elite football. It was not until the following year in Santiago, during a game against Universidad de Chile, that he began to find some form. In an encounter that was live on national television, he volleyed a shot into the roof of the net. São Paulo went on to win the competition.

Caine, more at home in horse-racing circles than on the South American football scene, received assistance from Argentine player agent Gustavo Arribas, once a partner in the HAZ player agency with Israeli dealmaker Pini Zahavi. It was Arribas who arranged Willian José's contract with Deportivo Maldonado. He would also handle other negotiations with a growing number of up-and-coming players that the club acquired – such as Alex Sandro, a Brazilian defender, and two teammates in Paraguay's Under-20 squad, Marcelo Estigarribia and Iván Piris.

Without playing a game in Deportivo Maldonado's humble stadium, Alex Sandro moved to Porto for a €9.6 million transfer fee and the Paraguayans fetched €1.2 million in fees when they moved on loan to Juventus and AS Roma. Typically, players involved in such deals through Uruguay would get 15% of the transfer fee under the arrangements – something that FIFA allowed, even if it was not in their regulations.

Caine told us by email that his interest in acquiring Deportivo Maldonado was in order to develop players. He said that Uruguay had produced some of the world's finest footballers, mentioning striker Luis Suárez who had gone on to play for Ajax, Liverpool and Barcelona. The club operated exactly like any other team, Caine said, and met all tax and other statutory requirements. "Our investment includes infrastructure, managerial, technical know-how, medical and other facilities as well as player development, training and players transfers," Caine wrote.

According to the club's chairman Federico Alvira, who handled the day-to-day running of the club, foreign investors were attracted to Uruguay by its tax regime. With little or no capital gains tax, it was a centre for offshore banking and known as the "Switzerland of South America". Lionel Messi, the four-time world player of the year, had recently set up a company in Uruguay to route income from his endorsement contracts. It was a legitimate arrangement, but Messi ran foul of the Spanish tax authorities for not declaring the revenue in the country where he lived.

Officials at the Uruguayan football federation were complimentary about Caine's buyout, even though some of the players Deportivo Maldonado signed never actually played for the club. Fernando Sobral, the federation treasurer, said that Caine was providing much-needed revenue for the club and praised the efficient way the club was run.

While Deportivo Maldonado's players were always paid on time, other club owners in the Uruguayan second division consistently paid players late or not at all. In some cases those footballers were in a situation that "bordered on indignity," according to the local player union boss. Many had to take a second job to provide for their families. They did not have medical insurance and their clubs did not have a doctor or physiotherapist if they got injured. They would have to travel to the union's headquarters for treatment.

In a late-night meeting, we spoke to a Uruguayan federation official in Zurich as he scoffed a plate of food on the terrace of the Renaissance Hotel on the eve of a FIFA meeting in 2015. "I don't see any problem with bridge transfers," he said. He was irked that some football executives in Europe disapproved of them. "The financial gulf between here and South America is so big and these operations are helping some of our clubs stay in business," he said.

In Brazil, the transfer of players like Willian José through Deportivo Maldonado barely raised a stir: moving young footballers through Uruguayan clubs had gone on since the 1980s and was regarded as standard procedure by sports reporters who covered player trading. "There's nothing secret going on here, nothing strange," club chairman Alvira said.

Despite flashes of brilliance, Willian José was struggling to become a consistent goal-scorer even if he was racking up more loan fees for Deportivo Maldonado. The website transfermarkt.com estimated that the club received $2 million from São Paulo and $3 million from two other first-division clubs, Gremio and Santos.

Willian was getting restless from being shifted around clubs without, he said, being given time to find his form and show what he could do. But then, in January 2014, it looked like he might have made a breakthrough. While relaxing on holiday back home in flip-flops, shorts and vest, his agent phoned from São Paulo to tell him he was on his way on loan to Real Madrid – or at least its second team Castilla. The move would allow Willian to mix with Cristiano Ronaldo and Gareth Bale.

It is a formidable transition from a holiday in the lazy days of Brazil's midsummer to the European winters when players are at peak fitness. Adapting to a different time zone and a new language, it was dizzying for Willian José. "The first time I went into the dressing room my head was spinning because everyone was speaking fast," he said.

Even so, after pulling on Real Madrid's white shirt for the first time for a match, he scored three goals in a 3-2 win in a 'B' team game at Recreativo Huelva in March. With Real Madrid's first team struggling in the league and Cristiano Ronaldo injured, coach Carlo Ancelotti promoted Willian to the first-team squad. He earned a place on the substitutes bench for a match at Celta de Vigo. But, wearing the No. 39 jersey, he got barely 20 minutes on the field in a 2-0 defeat and didn't get another chance during the rest of the season. His loan was not extended.

On a warm autumn evening on the outskirts of Madrid in October 2014, Willian was out on loan at yet another team, Real Zaragoza. It was his fifth stint on loan in as many years – a foil to the team's main striker in a match against Alcorcón. He held up the ball before laying it off for his teammate Borja "Baston" González, who scored twice in the 3-1 victory over the home team to maintain a promotion push. Willian and his teammates ran to one side of the cramped ground, to a few hundred Zaragoza fans in one corner. Like his companions, the Brazilian took off his jersey and handed it to one of the supporters.

A few days later, dressed in a grey cotton tracksuit and black baseball cap, Willian José was sprawled on a chair after training at Zaragoza's out-of-town grounds. He told us he was not happy with the way his career was going. Repeated loan moves had not given him time to settle down anywhere. He had not met Caine before but had complained to his agent, who had asked him to be patient.

At about the same time, Deportivo Maldonado turned its focus to two rising stars in Argentina. The club with 200 or so spectators at matches signed Gerónimo Rulli, a goalkeeper with Estudiantes de la Plata for a reported $4 million in 2014 and acquired Jonathan Calleri from Boca Juniors for as much as $12 million in 2016.

At 20 years old, Rulli had set a club record at the first-division team by going six games without conceding a goal. He told us that he travelled to Uruguay to sign a contract with Deportivo Maldonado, even if he didn't intend to play a game there. He was almost immediately loaned to Real Sociedad.

The 6-foot-2 goalkeeper won glowing praise from the Basque club's Scottish coach David Moyes for his debut season in La Liga. Moyes had been jettisoned by Manchester United and was trying to find his feet again in the north of Spain. In one match Rulli got the better of Gareth Bale when, in a one-on-one encounter with the winger, he blocked his shot.

Real Sociedad's board got rid of Moyes after just 12 months, but directors were determined to keep the young goalkeeper and signed him on loan for another year before making a move to sign him permanently the next year. Just as Real Sociedad officials were negotiating to pay some $8 million to Deportivo Maldonado for Rulli in the summer of 2016, Sheikh Mansour bin Zayed Al Nahyan's Manchester City stepped up and agreed to sign the young goalkeeper, according to the Spanish club's vice-president Angel Oyarzun. Then things got fuzzy. For some reason – one Basque newspaper even suggested it was uncertainty over the UK's decision to exit the European Union – Manchester City changed its mind about the deal. The club made no official comment, but Real Sociedad said it had agreed to immediately take Rulli back on loan from City and sign him on a permanent deal at the end of the year. City would maintain the right to buy him back in each of the next three summers, until he reached the age of 27.

On the southernmost tip of Spanish territory off the coast of Africa, Willian José had been making another new start at Las Palmas in the Canary Islands. It was his sixth loan move in as many years. The club had just been promoted to La Liga and wanted some firepower for its new campaign. The subtropical islands are the nearest point between Europe and Brazil and the climate, friendly locals and pace of life in Las Palmas were closer to his homeland than his previous placings in Madrid and Zaragoza. "I feel comfortable here," he said.

By scoring nine goals, many of them match-winning scores, the globetrotting Brazilian helped the team earn a respectable mid-table place in La Liga. According to website transfermarkt.com, his laggard market value had finally risen, doubling to €3 million in a single season. A few weeks later, he was on his way to Real Sociedad for a fee of as much as €6 million.

In the same week, according to *The Guardian*, Jonathan Barnett negotiated with West Ham for Calleri to join the London club on loan from Deportivo Maldonado.

Caine himself rarely travelled to Deportivo Maldonado's modest stadium for matches. The club remained in the second division, finishing third a couple of times but not doing enough to gain promotion. According to official documents released by European clubs and estimates by transfermarkt.com, the Uruguayan team earned about $40 million in transfer fees for half a dozen footballers who hadn't played a match there. When we exchanged emails in 2014, Caine said that he had not yet made a profit on his investment. By then, the transactions, while complying with football regulations, had started to attract the attention of a FIFA official in Zurich.

Chapter 8

"Todo Pasa"

A t 8.30 a.m. on a January morning, a bespectacled FIFA official is rushing to deliver a presentation close to the site of a new museum the football governing body is building near its headquarters in Zurich. The nine-storey tower, still a construction site clad in tarpaulin and iron scaffolding, is being prepped to become a showpiece of football memorabilia. Above it would be an apartment block, topped by swanky penthouses that would be marketed for rent for the equivalent of $8,000 per month. Around the official, commuters hop on and off trams that pass the sweeping granite façade of Bahnhof Enge railway station. Wearing a grey suit and carrying a briefcase, this Australian who heads FIFA's transfer monitoring agency has come to brief journalists about the latest player trading data in the international transfer market.

Mark Goddard had arrived in Switzerland in 2001 to work for FIFA on routine clerical tasks like hotel reservations, accreditation and ticketing. When his contract expired six years later, he was ready to pack his bags and return home. But then the world ruling body offered him the job of setting up a new online system that would log tens of thousands of international player transfers each year. It would be a clearinghouse for one of the most globalized employment markets in the world: few workers moved to the four corners of the world like footballers. Over the previous five years, South American players had been transferred to 122 of the 195 nations in the world.

The new electronic system was, Goddard said, a chance to improve the regulation of a marketplace in which massive quantities of cash flowed with little or no supervision. "Football is the last area of the commercial world where large amounts of money can be moved without oversight or regulation," Goddard had told a small group of reporters a few years earlier in an underground, soundproof room at FIFA's headquarters that was usually reserved for the meetings of senior executives. "It's been a jungle out there and that's about to change."

Goddard and his small team had jetted to 94 countries over the previous two years teaching clubs how to use FIFA's so-called Transfer Matching System, which was a slightly more complex version of a credit card transaction on Amazon.com. After abandoning the laborious process of sending faxes, the system allowed clubs to process a player move to another country in less than 10 minutes if the data submitted by the buying and selling team matched.

It was a new world for many in football. On his travels, Goddard said he had asked a team executive how he usually paid player transfer fees. The official pointed to a steel briefcase, intimating it was to carry bundles of cash. "I told him to tell his chairman that he wouldn't be able to do that anymore," Goddard said. With the new electronic system, clubs would have to log bank details of the money flow between clubs and agents. They would also have to upload a copy of the contracts.

As he arrived by tram for the 9 a.m. media briefing in a wood-beamed room next to the building site of the museum, Goddard ordered coffee and marvelled at the slickness of Zurich's public transport system. Most commuters in the Swiss city seemed to leave their car at home and as a result there were hardly any traffic jams. He was striving to make football transfers as efficient: over the previous few years, FIFA had acted like traffic cops by handing out more than a thousand fines of up to $15,000 to clubs for infractions such as not filing the correct paperwork.

Based in small rented offices down the hill from FIFA's head-quarters, Goddard managed a close-knit group of staff including legal director Kimberly Morris, a bubbly red-haired Canadian, and a collection of computer programmers and administrative staff. He said he also had a network of legal experts around the world to help him with compliance, although he would not give more details. Like Goddard, Morris was new to the intricacies of the football transfer market. She had worked as a commercial lawyer in London for Finers Stephens Innocent before joining FIFA in 2012. She too was enthusiastic to knock player trading into shape but, although they had a generous budget, their influence was limited to a certain extent. They could ask FIFA's disciplinary department to open cases but after that, they remained powerless.

Among the trades in their sights were the transfers through Uruguay that Juan Figer had pioneered in the 1980s. Goddard had visited Uruguay twice to warn clubs that the deals were no longer allowed. After his first visit, he was largely ignored. Kimberly Morris had more success in Zurich: she explained how the operations worked in a written explanation to FIFA's disciplinary committee. In a breakthrough, the committee agreed to take the unprecedented move of sanctioning one of the Uruguayan clubs, Atlética Sud América.

Sud América had registered six Argentine players for a few days without them appearing in a match. The players had been traded there by Argentine teams – Instituto Atlético Central Cordoba, Indepen-diente, Rosario Central and Racing Club – for what FIFA called non-sporting reasons. FIFA's disciplinary committee banned the Uru-guayan club from the transfer market for a year, and the Argentine clubs were fined between 15,000 and 50,000 Swiss francs. While the sanctions were small change in an industry where multi-million trades were commonplace, at least they showed FIFA was finally taking action.

But then Goddard suffered a reverse. Football's top tribunal, the Court of Arbitration for Sport, meeting in an 18th-century stately home Château de Béthusy outside the Swiss city of Lausanne, convened to consider an appeal by one of the three Argentine teams, Racing Club. The court appointed a panel of three lawyers to rule on the case: a long-haired Dane called Lars Hilliger, a Buenos Aires-born Israeli named Efraim Barak and Costa Rican football administrator Margarita Echeverria. Together, after considering the evidence presented by football's world ruling body they delivered a hammer blow verdict: "Nullum crimen sine lege."

Or, in other words, FIFA did not have an appropriate law to render illegal what some called "bridge" transfers. The judgement confirmed that there was a loophole in it's rules allowing a player to be registered with three clubs in a single season and only play for two of them. "The behavior that FIFA apparently nowadays consider to be a violation of its rules has been followed for years by several clubs all over the world, and FIFA has never manifested against it before," the panel said in a written ruling.

More than a decade earlier, in 2002, the Swiss court had made a similar statement to the one it was now issuing. Back then it overruled a FIFA committee which found that Argentina's Velez Sarsfield had acted "against the spirit and terms" of the regulations by only transferring 50% of a player's economic rights to Espanyol of Spain. "As long as FIFA rules do not issue an express prohibition, clubs are allowed to treat economic rights of players as assets and trade portions of them," the court said.

To stop such transfers, the 2015 panel advised FIFA to introduce a new law. There is, their written ruling said, nothing in the rules to stop transfers "with a purely economic purpose". The three arbitrators said that football's governing body should prepare a set of rules which, "in a clear and transparent manner", prohibit this type of player trading.

What Goddard could not do publicly was blame FIFA's South American executives who had not paid close attention to player transfers since the 1980s. The executives would meet in Zurich on FIFA business five times a year, staying in the five-star Baur au Lac hotel while picking up an annual stipend that had risen to as much as $300,000. They were among the men at the apex of the sport. They were chauffeured around town in black Mercedes-Benz limousines and made the key decisions like where the World Cup would be staged. Goddard, who went to work on public transport, was not in a position to criticize them.

Putting on a positive spin at the media briefing, Goddard said that the new online system had "turned the lights on" in the transfer market. FIFA's head of communications, Walter de Gregorio, joined Goddard for his presentation to ensure the Aussie with his dry sense of humour did not go off message when talking to the assembly of 25 journalists. Gregorio, a tall man who liked to wear aviator-style sunglasses, joshed with the reporters about making it in time a few hours after seeing them at the bar following the ritzy world player of the year awards won by Cristiano Ronaldo. Half an hour into Goddard's speech, the Ferrari-driving Swiss-Italian seemed bored. As Goddard paused for breath, Gregorio got up to bring an end to the briefing. "I haven't finished yet," snapped Goddard.

Goddard was not the only man looking to change the transfer system. The head of the Argentine tax agency, Richard Echegaray, was also putting pressure on FIFA to take action on what it called "sports tax havens" in South America. Argentine clubs were increasingly routing transfers through small teams in Uruguay and Chile, partly as a way to take dollars out of the country after the country's president Cristina Fernández in 2011 banned individuals and companies from doing so to protect the country's depleted reserves. That year, so-called capital flight had doubled to $22 billion as people sought a safe haven from the tumbling local currency, the peso.

Argentines quickly became jittery at the first signs of a financial crisis, following a 2001 monetary crisis when the government froze bank accounts. Back then, tens of thousands of people took to the streets beating pots and pans to demand access to their savings. Now, at the first signs of financial uncertainty, Argentines stashed dollar bills under their mattresses or in freezers at home. For clubs, footballers and their agents, routing transfers through foreign countries was a way to avoid the government's restriction on storing dollars abroad and it also reduced their tax burden.

The $1.7 million transfer fee for defender Jonathan Bottinelli was wired to a bank account in Miami when he went to River Plate via Union San Felipe, a Chilean team for which he never played, according to the tax agency. Echegaray's agency accused the player of tax evasion in a lawsuit in 2013, a claim that he has contested. Three years later, a trial was still pending at the slow-moving Argentine courts.

In 2014, the tax agency chief travelled to Zurich to tell FIFA president Sepp Blatter about a profusion of similar arrangements. Transfers, he said, had been routed through about a dozen clubs that included a tiny team in Switzerland, 42 miles from Blatter's home town of Visp in a valley below the Matterhorn. The transactions were, he told Blatter, depriving Argentina's treasury of millions of dollars of tax revenue.

FC Locarno was a spectacular drive through the foothills of the Alps from Visp, where Blatter still kept a weekend retreat. The Swiss team had acquired stakes of between 30% and 50% in the transfer rights of five players from River Plate, including striker Gonzalo Higuaín, for $13 million in 2006. The transactions were arranged two days before the end of the transfer window, and allowed the Argentine club to turn a profit for the year. José María Aguilar, the River Plate president, had shrugged when asked why the players had moved to such a small club. "They offered the most money," he said. "It's a little strange, but it's not our business to investigate."

Both FIFA and the Swiss football federation had approved the transfers, even though none of the quintet ever actually played for Locarno, which that year played to crowds of as few as 800 locals in the Swiss second division in a modest stadium overshadowed by the foothills of the Alps. The Stadio Lido had a single stand for spectators. There was a sand-filled long jump pit adjacent to one of the goals and a running track skirted the pitch.

The same year as Higuaín ostensibly signed for Locarno, he would instead play in front of sell-out crowds for Real Madrid at its 78,000-seat Santiago Bernabéu Stadium. The Spanish giant paid a transfer fee of as much as $16 million. FC Locarno's president Stefano Gilardi, a dermatologist whose son was the team sports director, said it was getting 900,000 Swiss francs (about $750,000) – money which helped him develop the youth team. Reached at his surgery by telephone, Gilardi said he didn't want to give any more details about the arrangement.

While Blatter's home town was not far away, one of his most senior executives probably had more intimate knowledge of the arrangement: Julio Grondona, the president of the Argentine football federation since 1979, was one of Blatter's closest aides on the world ruling body executive committee. With no interest in becoming FIFA president himself, Grondona had helped Blatter get elected, and was now one of the Swiss's chief supporters. When there was unrest among executives, the Argentine would interrupt: "Gentlemen, why are we arguing? The president is doing a fine job. Let's support the president."

The man whose first knowledge of accounting came from the books of his family's ironmongery in the Buenos Aires suburb of Avellaneda was now head of FIFA's finance committee. In 2010, it was Grondona that signed off on Blatter's bonus of 11 million Swiss

francs for overseeing the World Cup in South Africa. While he still
occasionally held court at the Formica tables of a motorway service
station his family also owned, Grondona's main domain was his third-
floor office of the Argentine federation. His desk was below a wooden
cross and a picture of himself with Pope John Paul II, who had started
his papacy one year before Grondona's reign.

Known as "Don Julio", or Sir Julio, Grondona was a supremely
dominant figure at the time. At the start of meetings, he would ask his
aides the time and they would shoot back: "What time do you want it
to be?" He wore a gold ring on his little finger with the inscription
"Toda Pasa", or "Everything Passes", which he said helped relax him
in tense situations.

Grondona had founded Arsenal de Sarandí – it took its name from
the London club – in Avellaneda in 1957, and its stadium now bore his
name. After becoming president of the Argentine federation, Grondona handed over the running of the club to his son Julio Jr., while he
became its honorary president. The club's officials had direct knowledge of the trading through Switzerland. On 25 August 2009, Arsenal
de Sarandí brought in midfielder Cristian Pellerano from Switzerland,
a country in whose league he had not played a match in his career.
Fourteen days later, a new official bulletin by the Argentine federation
Grondona oversaw showed that Pellerano had moved to another
Argentine team, Colón, again via Switzerland.

Grondona's early years as head of the federation had been
intoxicating. In 1986 he had overseen Argentina's second World
Cup title, with a thrilling display led by Diego Maradona. According
to critics, he and other Argentine football officials had little interest in
overseeing the business side of the game. "They are too often seduced
by success and sporting glory" said José María Aguilar, the River Plate
president. Grondona saw things differently. He said that he welcomed
the tax authority's investigation into so-called sports tax havens.

"We've always wanted transparency," Grondona said. "The federation is happy about what's happening."

Now aged 82, Don Julio was in a frail state and needed an electronic cart to ferry him around Zurich airport after arriving for FIFA business. After being helped into the limousine that delivered him to FIFA's headquarters, Grondona introduced Argentina's tax chief Echegaray to Blatter so that they could discuss the tax-avoiding operations. After showing him a replica of the golden World Cup trophy, Blatter promised he would look into the transfers and get back to him with more information.

Echegaray had also told the FIFA president of what he said were tax-avoiding transfers of Argentine players through Rangers de Talca, a second-division team in the capital of Chile's biggest wine-growing region, known for its Cabernet Sauvignon grape. Ricardo and Sebastian Pini had controlled Rangers de Talca between 2010 and 2014. The brothers signed Argentine defender Santiago Garcia and Colombian midfielder Carlos Sanchez to their modest club, which had not won a major trophy in more than a century.

In email exchanges with us, Sebastian Pini denied that he and his brother were avoiding tax or deliberately exploiting what the Court of Arbitration for Sport said was the loophole in FIFA's rules. He said they were mediators who, thanks to their knowledge of the global football business, had helped the two South American players by unblocking their career paths when they could not come to an agreement with the European clubs they played for: Palermo and Valenciennes. After selling their stake in the Chilean team, the brothers were pursuing another venture. They went to work on behalf of a group of investors in the USA and Switzerland to take over another minor club.

On their radar were Scottish first-division stragglers Motherwell and St. Mirren. Both were for sale. A week before Christmas 2014, Ricardo Pini, a man in his 40s with shoulder-length hair who had recently dated a blonde Argentine TV presenter, turned up at St. Mirren Park in Paisley, near Glasgow, to inspect the 8,000-seat stadium set in an out-of-town industrial estate. With its drab grey frontage, the unprepossessing six-year-old arena looks a bit like a storage warehouse, apart from one thing: the club crest showing it was founded in 1877. The chequered crest is based on Paisley's coat of arms. Pini was invited in through the tall glass doors to speak to St. Mirren directors. The club had a trading loss of £408,000 for the previous year and was an expensive if passionate pastime for its owners, including chairman Stewart Gilmour, who had typed "St. Mirren til I die" on his Twitter account profile.

The meeting helped both sides get to know each other, and St. Mirren director Bryan McAusland said that after a "wee look" at the Argentines they had seemed like decent enough guys. Pini also visited the club's training ground a few miles away, where he saw an Under-20 team game. He was shown a new white inflatable dome hoisted over artificial turf, on which players could train when snow, sleet and ice made the grass fields inhospitable. Two days later, Pini returned to watch last-placed St. Mirren lose 1-0 at home to Motherwell in front of 3,909 fans.

The St. Mirren fans who had missed pre-Christmas festivities to see their team lose to Motherwell and remain at the bottom of the first-division table were mystified by Pini's interest in their club. "I've got one simple question to these guys: why?" John White, the secretary of a supporter group, told the *Daily Record* newspaper. "If you do not have a St. Mirren background, then why are you here?"

By the end of January, Pini had turned his attention to Girona, a second-division team in northeast Spain. He invited Humberto Grondona, the other son of Don Julio, to watch the team play. Grondona worked as a sports director for Argentina's Under-20 team, after being appointed by the federation led by his own father. While he could not make the game, he said he was more than happy to offer

Pini advice about players. In the end, the Pini brothers gave up on acquiring a team in Europe and bought another Chilean team, Union La Calera.

In Zurich, FIFA administrator Goddard was no nearer to closing a loophole that had been exploited since the 1980s. There was nothing illegal in a player signing for a club and then leaving for another, for whatever career-planning reason might be involved.

Argentine tax chief Echegaray was also hamstrung by circumstances outside his control. He said that he had waited a year in vain for Blatter to assist him. He tried another approach: on another trip to Switzerland he visited Michel Platini, president of European ruling body UEFA, and asked for his assistance. Platini would, a few weeks later, announce that he planned to stand in the election to replace Blatter as president. The Frenchman was interested in helping. "If Blatter keeps his promise, that would be welcome," Echegaray said. "If it's Platini or whoever else becomes president, that would be welcome too."

Chapter 9

Buenos Aires to Manchester

I nvestment funds were emerging across Europe to service the demand for credit among clubs. Ray Ranson, a former Manchester City defender, had flirted with the business of transfer rights before the scandal involving the oligarchs and West Ham. From an office in Manchester, he was making a new push. "There are hundreds of millions of euros of demand out there" from European clubs, Ranson said. "The banks are shut."

His company, R2 Asset Management, could not operate in the English Premier League because of the ban that Richard Scudamore had implemented, but there were clubs willing to sell him the transfer rights of players in France, Spain, Denmark and Switzerland.

Other financiers followed suit. In Germany, banker Kai-Volker Langhinrichs raised €1 million to invest in the Bundesliga and hired Hamburg midfielder-turned-scout Harald Spörl to advise on which players to take a bet on. In Paris, Laurent Pichonnier, a partner of Fairplay Capital, sounded out the 20 clubs in the French first division. He said that all but Paris Saint Germain and Monaco were interested in doing business.

These fledgling funds, which were more sophisticated than many of the informal investment groups that operated in football, could trace their roots back to an initiative by Boca Juniors in Buenos Aires. La Boca, or "The Mouth", is the opening of the Riachuelo River and was the arrival point of many Spanish and Italian immigrants to Argentina. Its brightly painted houses and cobbled streets have since become a tourist draw, and tango dancers and painters come out during the day seeking business. After dark, the barrio is a far edgier place and guidebooks advise tourists against walking its streets. Murals on street walls show Diego Maradona holding his arms aloft in Boca's navy blue and yellow shirt and Marxist revolutionary Ernesto "Che" Guevara staring defiantly out at the rest of the world with a steely gaze. Rising up from the neighbourhood is La Bombonera, the "Chocolate Box" stadium where Boca plays had brought the teenage Maradona from Argentinos Juniors.

Seven years later, in 1982, Maradona fetched a world record fee of about $8 million when Boca Juniors traded him to Barcelona. But like in Brazil, such financial windfalls were unpredictable for teams. Boca did not know when they would next make a big sale to a European club. At the same time, Boca fans demanded success and supremacy against arch rival River Plate. So, Boca's presidents were pressurized into spending above the club's means to assemble the best team possible. To raise cash at short notice, Boca Juniors quietly cut deals to sell the transfer rights of players to businessmen. The opaque transactions would come out into the open when Mauricio Macri was elected president of the club in 1995.

The son of a successful businessman in the construction industry, Macri went to university to study civil engineering and then took a course at New York's Columbia Business School before working for his father and as a credit analyst at Citibank. One Saturday in 1991, Macri was bundled into a van outside his home in Buenos Aires by a gang of three men and driven to a house in the San Cristóbal district of the capital. Macri was held captive in a wooden box in the basement by his kidnappers. Without showing his face, one of the men – who called himself Mario – would come down the stairs with a flashlight each evening and hand him a bag containing a plate of takeout food through a tiny hatch in the box.

As other members of the gang threatened to kill him, Macri tried to create empathy with Mario so that they might take pity on him and spare his life. The two men talked about women and football. The young businessman said that his ambition was to become president of Boca Juniors, although he added "I don't know if I will be able to . . . well, I don't know if you are going to kill me". Mario responded with a smile, "how can we kill the future president of Boca?"

After 12 days in captivity, his father paid a $6 million ransom to release his son. On a Thursday night at 9.30 p.m., Mario dumped Macri, still bound and blindfolded, on a patch of wasteland and told him to bite through the rope to free himself. Ten minutes later he stumbled to a main road and hailed a cab to a friend's house and freedom. He would later say that the experience had given him a new determination in life. Macri used his father's contacts to become elected as president of Boca just as Maradona returned from Europe to play for the club at the age of 34.

Maradona's homecoming to Boca was spectacular. As he walked onto the turf at La Bombonera, the ground was engulfed by ticker tape and swirling navy blue and yellow smoke that matched the team's colours. A huge box was wheeled onto the pitch and opened in front of him to reveal his two young daughters dressed in Boca's kit. They held up a sign that said "Gracias Papá" and the 35-year-old Maradona began to weep. He sported a yellow stripe in his curly black hair and must have felt like the most loved man in Argentina, as thousands of fans chanted his name.

Macri's privileged upbringing and conservative views were not an obvious fit with Maradona, who had a tattoo of Ernesto "Che" Guevara on his right arm. The new president had begun to run Boca

Juniors more like a business at a time when European clubs such as Manchester United were starting to do the same. He cut payroll costs and built new VIP boxes to create revenue he would use to refurbish the rest of the stadium. At a pre-season meeting that lasted most of the night, Macri told the squad that he was cutting their win bonuses by 50%. The players, used to getting their way, were incensed. They yelled at him. "They were completely lawless," Macri later recalled.

Borrowing from an Argentine metaphor, Maradona said Macri – who at age 36 was less than two years older than him – had "less tarmac than Venice", because he was so inexperienced in football. "He's never been in a changing room in his life," Maradona spat. "Who is he to come and tell me we are going to pay you this much in bonuses."

At the time, Boca Juniors trailed arch rival River Plate, which plays 10 miles away at the Estadio Monumental. In Macri's first year in charge, River Plate won the Copa Libertadores, South America's top club competition. With no money to spend, Macri needed finance to reduce River's supremacy. He tried a different approach: he went to the stock-market regulator and said he wanted to set up a fund to trade on the stock exchange that would allow the public to finance the signings of Boca Juniors players in return for a share of their future transfer fees.

Macri's idea was that each of the fund's transactions would be made public. As he told the regulator his plans, they appeared anxious about the chaotic world of football coming into their more genteel environment. "You can imagine their faces," Macri said. "Between fear and terror." Macri persuaded them by putting up a $20 million bank guarantee.

The fund, La Xeneize Sociedad de Fondos Comunes de Inversion S.A., raised $14 million from some 1,500 investors to allow Macri to hire Martin Palermo, Nolberto Solano, Walter Samuel and Guillermo Barros Schelotto. La Xeneize means Genovese in the dialect of the Italian city of Genoa, where Boca Juniors' founders came from. The fund took stakes of between 48% and 84% in the transfer rights of the players.

There was a temporary hitch. Trading in the fund was suspended in its second year when an opponent of Macri complained that the president had broken Boca Juniors' statutes by taking a stake in the fund himself. Team rules said that the president himself could not profit financially from the club. The lawsuit was dismissed, after Macri pledged to donate any profit to charity.

While Macri was overhauling Boca's business model, Maradona was battling with what his agent Guillermo Coppola called a "daily war" with cocaine addiction. "He has some wins, some draws and some defeats," Coppola said. He had shown flashes of his old brilliance over two seasons during his Boca comeback, but after a league match against his first club Argentinos Juniors he tested positive for drugs for the third time in his career and – facing a doping ban – he announced his retirement on his 37th birthday.

Meanwhile, Macri's fund was turning into a successful gamble for investors. Solano joined Newcastle for about $2 million, Samuel moved to AS Roma for about $25 million and Palermo transferred to Villarreal in Spain for some $10 million. The transfers helped the fund to post a 32% return over four years through 2001, just as Argentina froze bank accounts amid one of its worst economic crises. Over the same four-year period, the Buenos Aires stock market plunged in value by 55%.

On the field, things were also working out and Macri could not resist revelling in the glory that came with breaking River Plate's dominance. In a two-leg 2000 quarter final, Boca Juniors came back from 2-1 down to score three goals in the last 15 minutes against River Plate and send its fans into delirium. Macri was so delighted that he walked, fully clothed, into the shower to join striker Martín Palermo. Boca Juniors went on to win the Libertadores Cup three times in the next four years.

Maradona remained unimpressed by Macri, who would go on to become Mayor of Buenos Aires and then, in 2015, president of Argentina. As president he appointed the player agent Gustavo Arribas, who worked on transfer deals for the British owner of Deportivo Maldonado, as head of Argentina's intelligence agency. Arribas reportedly ceded his role at the humble Uruguayan club to his own son, Ezequiel.

There would be no government role for Maradona, who remained at the other end of the political spectrum from Macri. He said that it had been his return to Boca – not the $14 million fund – that had lured so many star players. "I should have had a percentage" of the transfer fees of all the players Macri hired and then traded to European clubs for a profit, Maradona said. "I would give it to the Boca fans as a present."

On Rua Garrett, a cobbled street in the Chiado neighbourhood of Lisbon, a 28-year-old Portuguese banker had been inspired by the fund Macri created. Duarte d'Orey had a similarly privileged upbringing as the Argentine – heir to a shipping fortune, he had quit his job trading currencies and derivatives at Citibank in Lisbon in 1999 to apply his banking expertise to the family business. The fourth generation of a family with German roots, he stood out for his blue eyes and shock of blonde hair. He was aristocratic enough to make glossy society magazines, often on the arm of a glamorous girlfriend.

D'Orey and a group of young bankers set up First Portuguese Group, a fund management firm which raised money to bet on the rights of players at first-division clubs Sporting Clube de Portugal, FC Porto and Boavista. In cramped modern offices on a sloping street, D'Orey and his colleagues made up business cards which said that First Portuguese was regulated by the Bank of Portugal and the financial market regulator. It was an unusual sideline for the family business, which had entered shipping in 1886 to serve Portugal's trade routes with Brazil, Angola and Cape Verde. The company had transported goods to almost every corner of the world for 130 years. Now they were trading in footballers.

Portugal was one of the key entry points for South American players to Europe. Hundreds of Brazilian players left home every year to play abroad, and they could settle in Portugal more easily because they didn't need a visa or have to learn a new language. At the same time, Portugal, despite its small population, had an impressive record of producing top players like Luís Figo, the 2001 world player of the year who had matured at the academy of Sporting Clube de Portugal.

After raising €3 million, D'Orey bought a share of the rights of six Sporting players. Among them was a 17-year-old called Cristiano Ronaldo from the island of Madeira, who was trying to overcome bouts of homesickness in Lisbon. The fund paid some €627,000 for a 35% stake in the young prospect.

Sporting president Antonio Dias da Cunha craved the short-term financing that transfer market investors could bring.

The club was in a perennial battle with Portugal's two other heavyweight clubs, Benfica and Porto. Fans pored over their results and transfer targets in one or more of three sports newspapers that focused almost exclusively on football. As in Argentina, the presidents who ran the clubs on behalf of members had only a four-year term to succeed or face the axe and so were under pressure to achieve instant success.

D'Orey was onto a winner: the fund got €5.25 million of Ronaldo's transfer fee when the teenager was traded to Manchester United a year later – an 737% return on its money. Two other players the fund had invested in, Hugo Viana and Ricardo Quaresma, moved for big fees to Newcastle United and Barcelona, respectively. Overall, the First Portuguese fund increased in value by 85% in its first two years. Over the same period, Lisbon's stock-market index dipped 2%.

Porto was also hungry for cash, and in 2004 agreed to sell stakes in 10 players including Brazil-born midfielder Deco Souza for €6 million to a separate investment fund run by D'Orey. The team, led to the Europa League title the previous year by coach José Mourinho, had racked up €58 million in losses over the previous three seasons. To drum up investors, they held a roadshow at Porto's stadium and hired the club's former star player Paulo Futre as a pitchman.

A few weeks later, Mourinho's team helped Porto to the Champions League title with a 3-0 win against Monaco. With Jorge Mendes brokering the move, the coach was promptly hired by Chelsea's new owner Roman Abramovich and raided his former club for players; the fund's value swelled by 37% in barely four months.

Over five years through to 2004, D'Orey returned an average annual rate of 13% for investors via the Sporting, Porto and Boavista funds. Yet he was already looking for new investments outside football and would soon start winding the funds down, just as Ronaldo's and Mourinho's careers were taking off in London and Manchester.

As the financial crisis descended on Europe, Ray Ranson was among the new generation of hedge fund managers betting on the transfer market. As a teenager, Ranson had played in the 1981 FA Cup Final for Manchester City against Tottenham in an era before income from satellite television swelled the receipts of British football clubs. The match finished 1-1 and went to a replay that stands out for Argentine Ricardo "Ricky" Villa's dribble through the City defence under floodlights at Wembley Stadium; Spurs won 3-2.

Ranson's interest in finance was piqued on the team bus when he travelled to away games in his early 20s. On those journeys he would chat with insurance broker John Wilson, a wealthy fan who accompanied directors and mixed with them in the boardroom. After he moved on to Newcastle United from Manchester City, Ranson kept in touch with Wilson and they began an insurance business.

Since then his various career twists have seen him ally with the late Chelsea chairman Matthew Harding to raise £200 million of insurance-backed finance for British clubs, as well as having stints as owner of football data company Opta and as chairman of Coventry City. Now, Ranson was working on his latest venture from the eighth floor of a modern glass building among Manchester's neo-Gothic spires.

When we were invited to the offices of R2 Asset Management in 2013, we found a sports science graduate in his early 30s working on a computer in a sparsely furnished open-plan office adorned with black-and-white photographs of The Beatles. His expensive-looking black and silver business card said his name was Paul Smith and he was an analyst for the hedge fund.

Smith was not looking at investment products like stocks, bonds and currencies. His eyes were focused on the profile of Luciano Narsingh, a 22-year-old winger born in Amsterdam. Narsingh was coached at the Ajax academy that produced Johan Cruyff, Dennis Bergkamp and Frank Rijkaard, but he did not make it into the first team because at barely 60 kilos he was deemed too fragile. Now playing at rival PSV Eindhoven, he was starting to show that Ajax might have made a mistake in discarding him.

On his computer, Smith pulled up an eight-page file. According to his data, Narsingh was rated fourth of 80 wingers in the Dutch league, with a 69.9% score based on a variety of metrics such as the success rate of his passes and the number that led to a goal. That ranking made the grandson of Indian immigrants a possible investment opportunity for R2 Asset Management.

Using statistics to make decisions wasn't new in the City of London or even in football as Smith sat at his desk in 2013. Sam Allardyce's Bolton Wanderers had been using statistics since at least 1999 to find an edge in the transfer market. In his previous job, Smith was a data analyst at West Ham. What was novel was to use the same information to seek profits from the transfer market.

Ranson aimed to produce a 50% return on investment within two years. In line with many hedge funds, he would get a 2% management fee and 20% of the profits. Looking out of his floor-to-ceiling office window across the Manchester skyline, he pointed at the array of buildings. "The companies that own them can raise cash against their market value," he said. "That's all football teams are doing with their strongest assets – their players. We are not hunting for a jackpot by unearthing the next star player, we are providing a sophisticated financial service. We are higher up the food chain."

This type of talk riled European football bosses. Platini in particular was sick and tired of businessmen who were not directly involved in football "taking money out of the game". As a 17-year-old rookie, Platini was among the players to strike over a move by French club executives to unilaterally determine the length of their contracts. The players won. Five years later, before the opening match of the 1978 World Cup in Argentina, Platini and two older teammates led a protest over what they thought was their pitiful compensation for wearing Adidas boots. In response, the French national team painted over the three white Adidas stripes on their boots before they went out onto the field.

Now Platini was ratcheting up his criticism of the involvement of investment funds in public. Privately, the power of Jorge Mendes and a few other agents also rankled him and his aides. But to his frustration, FIFA was taking a more careful approach and had commissioned a second study of the transfer market by the Centre de Droit et d'Économie du Sport in Limoges, France. The study was taking months, more than 80 people were being interviewed and Platini was fearful that FIFA would end up doing nothing. "What will happen if FIFA does not act with sufficient consistency, energy and courage?" Platini fretted. "What will happen if the resolution, in the end, is neutralized by pressure from some investment funds blinded by the pursuit of profit?"

A few days later, he took matters into his own hands. UEFA's executive agreed to ban the practice within "three or four years" from its competitions, the Champions League and Europa League. That meant the likes of Atlético Madrid, FC Porto, Sporting Clube de Portugal, Besiktas and FC Twente would soon no longer be able to field players whose transfer rights were part owned by investment funds, if they wanted to continue receiving a share in more than $1 billion of UEFA prize money each year. Privately, fund managers scoffed at Platini, saying he didn't understand they were just providing financing agreements for clubs. They were not, they said, interfering with the market and controlling transfers.

Platini's determination to cut back on the rampant commercialism in football was well received by some of his compatriots in the French parliament. On the banks of the River Seine, at the 18th-century Palais Bourbon, Pascal Deguilhem, a 67-year-old deputy who was a former amateur rugby player, laid out his concerns to fellow parliamentarians. "Today, players meet up at the start of the season, change teams in January and go their separate ways at the end of the season," he said. The idea of a team representing a town had become redundant.

The lawmakers suggested measures – including one by Terra Nova, a Paris-based think-tank – that transfer fees should be scrapped altogether and players be treated like normal employees. Guénhaël Huet, mayor of a village of 8,000 people in the La Manche region of northern France, was most scathing in his speech about investors buying the transfer rights of players. It was as though they were trading in racehorses, he said.

Privately, Platini and other senior UEFA officials toyed with the idea of reforming the transfer market. The last time transfer rules were significantly altered was in 2001, six years after Belgian footballer Jean-Marc Bosman successfully changed the rules that allowed clubs to charge a fee for a player even after his contract had expired.

One morning the postman had dropped a letter into Bosman's postbox at the end of his neatly tended front lawn, next to where his snazzy Porsche Carrera was parked. It was from RFC Liège, the team he played for, and said that it was offering him a new contract that would cut his pay by 75%. Stunned, Bosman looked for a move to another team. He received an offer from Dunkerque, across the border in northern France, but the French club could not agree terms with Liège. Bosman was stuck and he went to court. After a five-year battle, the Belgian player won his case at the European Court of Justice, forcing FIFA to alter its rules. It took years of bartering to agree on a new set of regulations.

The court fight had left Bosman sidelined from football and now, in his 50s, he was jobless and living on benefits in the same suburban house. He had sold the Porsche long ago. He said that none of today's footballers had thought to contact him. "Not one of them has called me to say thank you," he said.

As transfer fees continued to rise, causing dismay among some observers, Platini's aides at UEFA looked at a new model that would tie fees to parameters like a player's salary and the number of years he had left on his contract. Their aim was to stop the inflation that was so attractive to investment funds. They drew up a proposal that would drastically reduce the biggest fees for the likes of Cristiano Ronaldo, who Real Madrid had signed for £80 million.

Under the UEFA proposal, which was not made public but circulated internally, fees would be linked to a player's salary: one of the sport's biggest names like Ronaldo, who was earning €10 million or more per year, would be traded for a fee of between €14 million and €28 million. A footballer earning a more modest €600,000 per year – a typical wage in English football's second-tier Championship – could only be transferred for between €300,000 and €800,000.

But the calculations, jotted down on a piece of A4 paper, were complicated and would be troublesome to implement. Leading European clubs were worried that an alternative to distributing football's wealth through transfer fees might erode their financial dominance. Imagine if they had to regularly share a cut of their television revenue among dozens of lower-division teams instead. At least with transfer fees, top clubs like Real Madrid, Manchester United and Bayern Munich retained autonomy over their wealth.

Stefan Szymanski, a sports business professor at Michigan University who has co-written a book about football called *Soccernomics*, said there was a strong case for changing transfer rules because so little of the fees trickled down to clubs in lower leagues. Earning transfer money was like playing the lottery for smaller teams, he said. It was "remarkable" that neither UEFA nor any other football authority had attempted to produce a scientific study on how to maintain competitive balance in the game.

Without making the plans public, UEFA's back-of-the-envelope calculations about altering the regulations did not go any further, apparently because it was too complicated to make any changes. The 125-year-old transfer system may not have been perfectly designed, but it would be highly tricky to overhaul. It was a bit like the London Underground train network, started in 1894. The transport system was in need of an upgrade, but any effort to bring it up-to-date in one sweeping move would cause no end of complaints and disruption. It was far easier to tinker with the existing model.

As one of the game's senior statesmen, Platini had other ways of exerting influence on how the market operated. He controlled the money-spinning Champions League and the European Championship, the national team competition held every four years. The two competitions generated billions of euros in television revenue and sponsorship. Among the businesses angling for a cut of this revenue was CAA, the Beverly Hills-based company that managed an investment fund led by Peter Kenyon, the former Manchester United and Chelsea chief executive.

The fund had acquired stakes in players from Lisbon-based Sporting, among other clubs.

Some of the young footballers at Sporting were represented by Mendes who, according to Kenyon, was to be paid a commission when the fund made money on transfers. Critics said it wasn't right for an agent to act for a player and also have an interest in his transfer rights. FIFA examined Mendes's involvement with the CAA investment fund but did not even question him, let alone take any action, according to a person familiar with the case. Kenyon, speaking from CAA's office in London's Hammersmith, said the fund was "very conscious" that it should not interfere with player trading. "We've been aware of conflict and we've managed that conflict," Kenyon said. Kenyon said that Mendes's career showed he wasn't interested in a quick profit. "He's developed players in conjunction with their clubs," Kenyon said. After all, his biggest client, Cristiano Ronaldo, had spent six years at Manchester United.

However, pressure from Platini appeared to pay off. CAA, which had recently won a contract to manage the marketing rights of the 2016 UEFA European Championships in France, said it was disposing of the transfer market fund and it was clear where its priorities now lay: it set up an office a mile away from UEFA's headquarters on the banks of Lake Geneva.

Chapter 10

"I Want 40% for the Boy"

As he rode his horse around his enormous country estate in the bright sunshine of the plains of central Spain, Miguel Ángel Gil mulled over the next step for Atlético Madrid. He had borrowed from investment funds and wealthy individuals to keep creditors at bay, and assembled a squad to win the club's first La Liga title in 17 years, but he was tired of the financial balancing act he had to perform. He wanted a longer-term plan. He looked enviously at Real Madrid and Barcelona, who could command huge television deals and sponsorships. They had annual revenue topping €500 million, more than three times what Atlético earned.

Barcelona, wowing football fans with attacking displays led by Lionel Messi and supported by Xavi Hernández and Andres Iniesta, had recently snagged a €30 million per year deal with Qatar to brand its burgundy and blue shirts with the Gulf state's name. Real Madrid was in talks with Abu Dhabi about the naming rights of its Santiago Bernabéu Stadium that would help finance a €400 million refurbishment, including a money-spinning hotel and shopping centre.

Even as the newly minted Spanish league champion, Atlético Madrid could not attract the backing of such rich allies because it did not have the big names that its bigger rivals had: players like Messi and Cristiano Ronaldo. The Atlético players were a bunch of outsiders, even if as a group they were formidable. Defender Filipe Luís described the team under the black-suited coach Diego Simeone as like the fictional motorcycle club in the *Sons of Anarchy*, a television series loosely based on the Hell's Angels. In the American crime series, the group of bikers have an unbreakable bond.

In Atlético's cast was assistant coach Germán Burgos, a former goalkeeper from Argentina who had once played in a heavy metal band. He even had his own nickname – "Mono" or "Monkey" – like the characters in *Sons of Anarchy*. His weight had ballooned since he quit playing for Atlético Madrid in 2004, after helping the team win promotion back to the first division. Lounging around in Madrid, he spent his days playing five-a-side football, with the occasional gig as a football pundit on Spanish TV. Simeone gave his friend a new lease of life, hiring him as an assistant first at Racing Club de Avellaneda in Argentina and then at Atlético.

So, how could Miguel Ángel Gil try to find another way to bring his loveable but motley crew into the money and wean the club off its reliance on short-term loans? He turned to two of the emerging countries that investment bank Goldman Sachs had coined BRIC nations: India and China. Seeing untapped potential in their combined 2.6 billion population, Gil began exploring ways to plant seeds that might one day bring Atlético Madrid the standing that Real Madrid and Barcelona enjoyed around the world. He opened talks on co-owning a football team in India and had started to make regular trips to China for discussions about how Atlético could help the government's plan to make the world's 97th-ranked national team a power in the sport. It was a project that would need months of careful diplomacy.

Like Real Madrid, Barcelona did not have to try so hard to get attention on the global stage. Barça was already an established brand, and by hiring star players could bring themselves tens of millions of euros in extra marketing revenue. For several years now the two superpowers had their eyes fixed on a young player from Brazil, who they realized could be a gold mine for them. The next Messi, or the next Ronaldo. Or even the next Pelé.

On a July evening in 2011, the football world's focus was on the Vila Belmiro Stadium in Santos, which appears little changed from the days in 1965 when a teenage Pelé lived in a dormitory under one of the stands. National-team coaches had arrived in Brazil ahead of the World Cup qualifying draw, as a 19-year-old footballer called Neymar went toe-to-toe with Ronaldinho, a two-time world player of the year famous for his hip-swivelling trickery with the ball and toothy grin.

Sporting a blond mohawk hairstyle that teenagers all over Brazil were copying, Neymar was a blur of energy and movement. He danced past six players before slipping the ball into the net. One of the moves was so rapid that it required slow-motion replays to understand just how he had done it. "Sensational" British football writer, Henry Winter, told his 1 million Twitter followers.

News of the boy playing for Pelé's former team had spread beyond Santos six years before. Like the goods loaded onto ships that set sail from the port city, Neymar had become a commodity that the biggest clubs in the world wanted. His agent Wagner Ribeiro had moved Santos's previous star, Robinho, to Real Madrid at age 21 for $30 million. The next year, Ribeiro took the 14-year-old Neymar to see the world's richest club.

When Santos found out, it became worried that Neymar, who it didn't yet have tied to professional terms, would sign as a free agent with the Spanish club. Santos executives contacted football lawyer Marcos Motta and asked him to warn off Real Madrid and alert the football authorities. "We said: listen he's a minor," Motta said. "We called FIFA, we called the Brazilian football federation – we called everybody." Real Madrid said Neymar was just visiting. Soon after, Neymar signed his first contract with Santos.

Like most clubs in Brazil, Santos could not match the wages top European teams were offering. So, when Neymar renewed his contract soon after signing an initial deal, his agent managed, as an alternative, to convince Santos to give Neymar 40% of his future transfer fee. It was not unheard of for South American footballers to receive the promise of a cut of their next transfer fee. It was a way for clubs to retain talent a season or two longer. FIFA allowed club executives to award players up to 15% of their own fees (in 2015, in an internal directive, FIFA effectively capped the amount at €1 million) – what was more unusual was for a player to bank a cut of his transfer rights before he was even traded.

But Neymar was not an ordinary player, and his agent Wagner Ribeiro knew it. "Wagner said I want 40% for the boy", Motta, the Santos lawyer, said. "So Neymar got 40%." Santos sweetened the deal by telling Neymar's father it had arranged an immediate buyer for the stake: supermarket chain owner Delcir Sonda.

Sonda's chain of 24 supermarkets in São Paulo was pulling in 2 billion reais a year and he had already paid a little more than €1 million to buy portions in the rights of a group of five other Santos players. As usual there was a tussle over the price he would pay. Neymar's father valued the stake in his son's transfer rights at 5 million reais, the equivalent of about €1.8 million. For some of Sonda's advisors that was too much for a 17-year-old, according to Eduardo Carlezzo, a lawyer who was working for Sonda. "Thousands of players that are great hopes when they are 16 or 17 end up not making it." But in meetings at Sonda's offices in São Paulo, one thing became plain: Neymar's father, who led negotiations on behalf of his son, held all the aces in this poker game. Sonda agreed to pay the 5 million reais demanded and even came up with an extra $500,000 for Ribeiro, the agent. Neymar therefore become a millionaire while many of his peers were still at school.

A few years earlier, Neymar's father, who had the same given name as his son, had been juggling careers as a semi-professional football player and car mechanic. He shared a room with his wife, daughter and son in São Vicente, a satellite town close to Santos. Like many Brazilians, the family went to the local Christian Evangelical church. Although, at 12, Neymar lacked the strength and size of boys even his own age, he would outclass those who were several years older. One match at a church camp stuck out for the pastor's son, Newton Lobatto Netto. "There was a guy, he was a really good goalkeeper and Neymar just humiliated him," he said. By then Neymar was already playing for the local boys' team at Santos. Antonio Lima dos Santos, a trainer at the club and once a teammate of Pelé, says he first saw the 13-year-old kid playing "futebol de salão" – literally meaning living-room football – an indoor game with a heavy ball where poise and quick thinking are more important than power.

Neymar was running rings around his rivals and making the game look so easy that Dos Santos felt the boy should be tested against older opposition. He suggested this to Zito, a one-time mentor of Pelé who had played with him in two World Cup-winning teams and was now a club director. "Zito told me I was mad," Dos Santos recalls. "You can't do this. He's very skinny, very weak," Lima recalls. Neymar readily accepted the challenge and flourished. Sometimes his confidence would spill over into arrogance and his coaches had to step in. "He could go over the limit," Lima said. "But we asked him to correct it and he did."

With Neymar reaching manhood, his father controlled one of the most appreciating assets in football. As soon as his son had agreed to sign professional terms, Santos offered him a five-year contract. Santos arranged a signing ceremony but, with journalists crammed into a room at the club's headquarters, the deal almost unravelled in a sign of the tumultuous nature of Brazilian football. "We arrived believing everything was set and that all that was left to do was sign the agreement," Carlezzo, Sonda's lawyer, said. "Then the vice president of Santos started to claim 'no we cannot sign this!' He was red, red! I think he almost had a heart attack."

"I turned to the president of Santos and said, if you agree to changes your guy is proposing we are not authorized to sign the deal.

Then we are no longer buying this 40% and Neymar would not sign this five-year deal. The president turned to me and said we have to sign."

The next day, Neymar made his professional debut for Santos, coming on for the last 30 minutes of a state championship game. He wore a jersey several sizes too big that hung loosely off his child's frame. Fans were already chanting his name before he came onto the pitch. His earliest touches had the crowd on its feet. "The boy set fire to the game," said one report. Santos won 2-1. Neymar went on to score 10 goals in his first league season and 17 in the next, and there were more wealthy investors lining up for a piece of his future transfer rights. A group of wealthy Santos fans bought 5% of those rights from the club through Terceira Estrela Investimentos ("Third Star Investments"). Their 3.5 million reais outlay meant Neymar's perceived transfer value had soared more than fivefold in a year.

For supermarket owner Sonda and his investment advisors, the focus now was on continuing to cultivate a relationship with Neymar's father and trying, with his consent, to secure a big profit by promoting the idea of transferring Neymar to a top European team. Trips to Europe became commonplace.

Carlezzo says a Sonda executive told him of a meeting between Neymar Sr. and Chelsea owner Roman Abramovich in London. Though Neymar was just beginning his career, his performances were such that Brazil coach Dunga started to come under pressure from sections of the media to include him in his squad for the 2010 World Cup. After all, wasn't Pelé just 17 when he helped Brazil win its first World Cup in 1958? In the end, Dunga left Neymar at home. Brazil exited the tournament with a quarter-final defeat to the Netherlands and Dunga lost his job.

Six months later, Neymar made his debut for Brazil in a friendly game against the USA to mark the opening of the Red Bull Arena in

New Jersey. On the same day, Chelsea made an offer to sign him. "We had a meeting in the Hilton Hotel on Lexington Avenue" in New York, Motta, the football lawyer said. Seated in the lobby were a large group of interested parties: Neymar's father, his agent Wagner Ribeiro, Pini Zahavi, the Israeli dealmaker who knew Abramovich, a delegation from Chelsea and Luis Álvaro de Oliveira Ribeiro, the newly elected Santos president. "Neymar's father started to play his game, saying he might go or not. It will depend, let's see," Motta said. "He started to realize he could get a very interesting contractual situation for the boy with Santos. He had control."

Luis Álvaro ended the conversation quickly. He rejected the €35 million being offered by the Premier League team. While he tried to appear calm, he was spooked by Chelsea's push to sign Neymar immediately. He phoned officials back in Brazil to prepare a special career-plan programme designed to keep Neymar at the club for as long as possible. The plan included giving him English and Spanish lessons, specialist physical preparation and hiring him a wealth-management team.

Luis Álvaro also spent time trying to persuade Neymar to develop fully as a player before leaving for European football. Over a four-course lunch with the authors at his penthouse apartment in São Paulo that finished with lemon meringue pie, the club president used Brazil's ubiquitous "churrasco" (barbecue) as a metaphor to describe his point of view. "It's the same thing as putting a steak on the grill. If the meat is uncooked you have to leave it 10 minutes and then you'll have the best beef. Neymar was uncooked meat at 19 years old."

Luis Álvaro managed to hold on to the teenager. Neymar led Santos to South America's top club competition, the Copa Libertadores, for the first time since 1963 when Pelé was in the team. Neymar had scored throughout the run to a two-legged final against Peñarol. He opened the scoring in the decisive second game, where a 2-1 victory clinched the championship, and was named man of the match.

His bargaining position now stronger than ever, Neymar's father persuaded the Santos president to sign what some saw as a naïve agreement by the club allowing its star player to negotiate a future transfer with four years left on his contract and leave one year earlier than planned.

The licence to negotiate with other teams, set out in a brief one-page letter, meant the father could go to the market early to drum up interest and he subsequently listened to offers from Barcelona, Real Madrid and Bayern Munich. The end goal for the Neymar entourage was for Neymar to remain at Santos until the 2014 World Cup, when he and his sponsors – such as Nike, Red Bull and Panasonic – would capitalize on his profile before he moved to Europe.

Real Madrid was well aware of the array of sponsors that Neymar was attracting. The Spanish club had a policy of taking 50% of endorsement deals players signed, and for years had pursued high-profile players such as David Beckham to increase its income. José Ángel Sanchez, the club's general director who had signed Beckham in 2003, had a meeting with Sonda lawyer Eduardo Carlezzo in Madrid in late 2011. At about the same time, Real Madrid made a €45 million bid for Neymar but it was rejected, and the lawyer representing the supermarket chain owner was powerless to help push the move through. "I told Real Madrid we would be interested for the player to come to Real Madrid as well, but the influence Sonda has over Santos is near to zero," Carlezzo said. Sonda's relationship with Santos had deteriorated because the club no longer liked the idea of outsiders sharing in Neymar's transfer fees, and had "started a war" with Sonda, Carlezzo said.

Real Madrid tried another front. President Florentino Pérez called his Santos counterpart while the Brazilian was taking the two youngest of his six children on a trip to France. Pérez offered to fly Luis Álvaro to Madrid for lunch. "I imagine you want to have lunch with me to talk about Neymar's rights?" Luis Álvaro said, recalling the conversation. "I said 'don't waste your time and fuel on the plane because we have no interest in selling.' What did he do? He got on his jet, flew to Paris and had lunch with me." Over rack of lamb and potato gratin at Guy Savoy, one of the most exclusive restaurants in Paris, Álvaro told Pérez what he had told Chelsea: no sale.

Still, Real Madrid felt like it was making progress with Neymar's father. Motta even drew up a contract between the club and Neymar. The deal was to be done in top secret, though with time running out before a crucial meeting, Motta had to complete his work on the one-hour TAM airline flight between Rio de Janeiro and São Paulo. "I said to my assistant Stefano, let's go over the contract on the plane," said Motta, an extrovert who sports dress shirts bearing his initials. "But we won't take the first page of the contract because you never know who's sitting next to you."

The next morning at 5 a.m. he received a call on his mobile phone from a friend asking him if he'd seen that morning's O Globo newspaper. In the pages of the Rio de Janeiro-based daily, columnist Anselmo Gois noted: "Marcos Motta the lawyer of Neymar was on the TAM flight in the morning revising a contract between Real Madrid and the boy." Motta thought back to who might have been looking over his shoulder on the flight. "There was a guy pretending to sleep, a kind of famous guy from TV and maybe he saw," Motta said. "I was concerned about people behind us, not about this guy that looked like he was sleeping." In the end, the draft contract wasn't needed.

Roman Abramovich had not given up wooing Neymar either. Michael Emenalo, a former Nigerian player who was Chelsea's director of football, flew to Santos to try again. He met Neymar in the port city and proceeded to deliver one of the best sales pitches Motta had ever heard. "It was the very first time that I saw Neymar's father listen to someone for more than 30 minutes without looking at his mobile," Motta said. Emenalo told the story of the Chicago Bulls and Michael Jordan. How Chicago was not a big team, but together they evolved into international icons. Neymar could become Chelsea's Michael Jordan, Emenalo said. José Mourinho was about to return to the club as manager and he wants to sign you, the Nigerian added. "You are going to lead Chelsea to the top."

Zahavi, the Israeli agent, was not far away from the action. He had called Motta to say that he was on his way to Brazil to sort out the transfer of a player he refused to name by phone. After arriving in São Paulo, Zahavi confided to the lawyer that the footballer was Neymar. There was a problem, Motta told him: Zahavi would be encroaching on the territory of Wagner Ribeiro, the player's agent. Motta arranged a meeting to try and reach a solution where Zahavi could be shoe-horned into the negotiations. The meeting place was the Emiliano Hotel in Rua Oscar Freire, São Paulo's swankiest shopping street where boutiques pump perfume out into the street to lure wealthy Brazilians in to buy designer brands.

In the hotel's small lobby, the Israeli met with Wagner Ribeiro and representatives from Sonda and even Neymar's church to make a game plan. It was a noisy discussion, a real bagunça – "a mess" – Motta said. But eventually they agreed on an unusual compromise. Ribeiro and Zahavi would divide up representation of Neymar in Europe depending on their sphere of influence.

Also seeking a cut of any future transfer fees was the Milan-based agent Giovanni Branchini, who made an initial approach to Neymar on behalf of Bayern Munich. The more he met with his son's powerful suitors, the more money Neymar's father realized he could extract from them. He decided that whichever team wanted to sign his son would have to pay an upfront fee of €10 million, an arrangement that was unheard of in world football. And then, upon completion of the deal, his son would be due a further €30 million. Under the plan, if either side reneged, it would be liable to pay a €40 million penalty. Motta told Neymar Sr. it was a masterstroke. "I said: congratulations you are there. It's not a matter of money now. You can get the money you want from Chelsea, Real Madrid, Barcelona or Bayern. It's time for you to look in your son's eyes and say where do you want to play, what makes you happy?"

Neymar's father, acting on the advice of his wealth advisors, took out an insurance policy to protect his son against paying €40 million in case he was seriously injured before his transfer to Europe. Barring a hitch, the former car mechanic had played the transfer market as effectively as any hedge fund.

Chapter 11

The Pharmacist's Medicine

According to his inner circle, there was only one team Neymar had his heart set on playing for: Barcelona. Coached by Pep Guardiola and led on the field by Lionel Messi, the Catalan club had beaten Manchester United 3-1 at Wembley Stadium in May 2011 taking its third Champions League title in five years, cementing a period of dominance not seen for years. Alex Ferguson, the losing side's manager, said it was the best team he had faced in his 40-year career. Of Andrés Iniesta and Xavi Hernández, the axis of the team in midfield, Ferguson said they passed the ball so fast and accurately it made your head spin. After his team had lost 4-1 at Barcelona the previous season, Arsenal coach Arsène Wenger said Messi's magnetic control of the ball was as though he was a player in a PlayStation video game. As the plaudits lined up, Neymar was sure he wanted to be part of this football dynasty.

Barcelona president Sandro Rosell, who had worked in Brazil as a Nike marketing executive, asked Brazilian André Cury to lead negotiations with Neymar and his father. The pitch was a simple one: "Do you want to play for the best team in the world?" Real Madrid had delivered messages to Neymar from Cristiano Ronaldo and Jose Mourinho, but the introverted Lionel Messi never dropped a line or sent a message encouraging the teenager to join him. Perhaps it wasn't necessary. Neymar was only 19 and had only recently moved out of the one-bedroom family home when he secretly agreed to join Barcelona. On 15 November 2011, Neymar signed a deal pledging to join Barcelona in 2015, and in return the club would pay him an initial €10 million and a further €30 million when he moved. Three days later, Neymar's parents formed a company called N&N Consultoria Esportiva e Empresarial to receive the first payment. Ten million euros were wired into its bank account in São Paulo.

The pact wasn't made public and not even Santos knew about it. Eight months later, Barcelona buried the terms of the deal on page 178 of its financial accounts, saying it had made a down payment on a future purchase without giving any more details or mentioning Neymar's name. Santos president Luis Álvaro de Oliveira said that the first he knew of the agreement was when O Globo published the details two years later.

Having signed the secret deal with Barcelona, Neymar's father continued to exert pressure over Santos by requesting it shorten his son's contract by one year to 2013. Barcelona wanted to bring forward the deal, because Real Madrid was still pushing aggressively to sign Neymar. Real was offering him a higher salary and offered to pay the €40 million he would be liable to pay Barcelona for rescinding their deal. Barcelona reminded Neymar that he would have to share half of his pay from new sponsorship contracts with Real Madrid.

Barcelona won the tussle and negotiated what appeared to be a very modest €17 million transfer fee with Santos. It was a personal victory for the Barcelona president Sandro Rosell. The handsome son of a former club director, he was a member of the Catalan establishment and was reported to have a fortune of €250 million that included petrol stations and property. A decade earlier, Rosell had boasted how as vice-president he had persuaded another Brazilian star, Ronaldinho, to join Barcelona ahead of Manchester United. Beating Real Madrid to Neymar was an even bigger coup. Clean-shaven and dressed in a dark-blue suit and check tie, Rosell hugged Neymar at the signing ceremony and chatted amiably to him in fluent Portuguese. But the taste of success would not last long for the president. At about the same time, Rosell was making an enemy among the team's fans.

Jordi Cases, a pharmacist in his 40s from a town outside Barcelona called Olesa de Montserrat, had a season seat in the cheap third tier at the Camp Nou stadium that cost a few hundred euros a year. Cases had become incensed by a decision by Rosell to sign a €30 million-a-year sponsorship deal with Qatar to replace children's charity Unicef. Prior to the Unicef deal, the club had never had a brand name on it shirts. He felt that Rosell and his board were betraying the motto of being "més que un club" (Catalan for "more than a club"). The words were painted onto the seats at the 98,000-seat Camp Nou stadium.

Presented by Rosell as a way for Barcelona to stay competitive in the Champions League against superpowers such as Bayern Munich and Manchester United, the Qatar sponsorship was approved by just 697 Barcelona members with voting rights at the previous annual general meeting. Cases said the sponsorship was such a significant development that all of the members should be consulted. He and some friends set up a pressure group to try and force a new ballot of all 170,000 members. The motion failed to get enough signatures.

Barcelona is in theory controlled by its members: it's they who elect the president and the board every year. But Cases was irked by the lack of say the members had once the election was over. After failing to make headway with the decision to put Qatar's name on the team shirts, he turned his attention to page 178 of the club's financial report that mentioned a €10 million down payment on a €40 million accord. Was this to Neymar? He wrote to Rosell and the board seeking more details. They ignored him.

In December, Cases faxed a complaint to Spain's National Court in Madrid asking it to investigate whether Rosell had misapplied funds to make the payment. He said that he wasn't accusing the president of a crime, he just wanted to know how the club was spending money on behalf of members.

The board responded to Cases this time. Rosell called the complaint "reckless" and his general secretary, Tony Freixa, wrote a letter in Catalan on Christmas Eve to the family pharmacy saying the club could seek damages from him if confidential details about Neymar's contract were made public. "As you can imagine, the size of the damages would be very high," Freixa wrote.

Cases was unbowed – defiantly, he would add the words "reckless and imprudent" to his Whatsapp profile. When, after the Christmas break, judge Pablo Ruz agreed to investigate, Cases realized he had triggered a scandal. Rosell immediately quit as president, although he continued to deny wrongdoing. He said he was stepping down to stop the fallout affecting the club.

After receiving permission from Neymar's family to speak in public, Barcelona called a press conference. With PowerPoint slides, interim president Josep Bartomeu, who had stepped in to replace Rosell, said the transfer was costing the club €57.1 million – the €17.1 million Santo transfer fee plus Neymar's €40 million – although there were a series of bonus payments worth millions more to the player and his family. Neymar would receive €500,000 per year to be a so-called ambassador for Barcelona in Brazil and his father would receive €400,000 per year to scout three young Santos players. All the payments were on top of Neymar's annual salary of more than €10 million. "We can't be any more transparent," Bartomeu told reporters after the two-hour news conference.

Public prosecutor Jose Perals accused Barcelona of financial engineering by drawing up as many as nine separate agreements to avoid the club paying €12 million in tax. Barcelona should have withheld 25% of all payments to Neymar as income tax on non-residents, he said. Five days later, Barcelona paid €14 million to the tax authorities to cover a possible shortfall plus interest. At the same time it maintained its innocence, saying that it had acted on the advice of tax experts. That wasn't enough to get off the hook: the judge ruled there was enough evidence for Rosell to stand trial for "crimes against the public treasury" and for "dishonest" management. Cases, the pharmacist, had not intended to make such an impact and he withdrew his complaint from the Madrid court. It was too late. The court case was going ahead and Rosell faced up to seven years in prison if convicted.

Neymar's father, who was now enjoying the wealth he had negotiated for his family, said he had done nothing wrong. He wasn't charged with any crime and said he had paid all taxes due in Brazil. Dressed in a white shirt, purple tie and suit and carrying a black Louis Vuitton briefcase, the former mechanic turned up at court in Madrid to give evidence to judge Ruz, winking and flashing a thumbs-up sign to press photographers.

In Brazil, he rebuffed claims by Sonda, the supermarket chain owner who had paid him about €1.8 million for 40% of Neymar's transfer rights, that he should get a bigger return on his investment than 5 million euros. The wealthy investor argued that the deal was structured to keep the transfer fee low and reduce his share of the money.

Neymar's father said that Sonda had no reason to complain. He had received a return of almost 280% on his original investment. If he'd invested in the Brazilian stock market, he would only have got a return of 21% over the same three-and-a-half-year period. If he had invested in dollars to gain in value against the Brazilian real, he would be sitting on a loss. Neymar Sr. said that all he had done was negotiate the future rights of his son, the prodigy who was emerging as a global superstar on a par with David Beckham at a time when football was bigger business than ever. He was leveraging demand in the same way businesses did. "Can't a club negotiate its future television rights? Or a farmer negotiate on the price of his harvest before planting his crops?" the former mechanic said. "Those are simple analogies to explain the business model we used."

As Barcelona grappled with the scandal, Atlético Madrid owner Miguel Ángel Gil was enjoying a relatively peaceful time thanks to the finance he had negotiated with a new group of lenders. However, he continued to look for more long-term backing. As part of a deal with billionaire Wang Jianlin – China's richest man – Gil had welcomed 20 Chinese schoolchildren between the ages of 13 and 15 to the club. The youngsters, who had never travelled abroad before, had arrived wide-eyed at Madrid's Barajas airport dressed in suits and ties, and posed for a photograph with tiny Chinese and Spanish flags. In a talent sweep of the country, they had been identified for their athletic skills at individual sports like table tennis and badminton. Football was barely played in Chinese schools, although the government was trying to change that. After all, football diplomacy had the potential to be far more powerful than the so-called ping-pong diplomacy of the early 1970s, when the Communist state had invited the American table-tennis team to visit.

Wang, chairman of the Dalian Wanda Group, was buying up property in London and film studios in Hollywood as part of an international push by China. He was also among the business elite who had been entrusted by the Chinese government to develop football in the world's most populous country, whose national team was ranked world no. 97 by FIFA, below the likes of Benin, Guinea and Guatemala. Chinese vice-premier Liu Yandong approached Wang. "Comrade Yandong spoke to me in person, hoping that I would take the task to help rebuild Chinese football", Wang said before the children were dispatched to Atlético in 2011.

Spain, which had recently won the World Cup, had been identified as the best place for Chinese children to hone their skills. Two other groups of 20 children were sent to Valencia and Villarreal, clubs in the east of Spain. Under the three-year deal, each club would get €3 million. That was a valuable contribution to Atlético Madrid's finances, but Gil also saw the possibility of more cooperation with

Wang Jianlin that could make the team part of the nascent boom in football in a country of 1.4 billion people.

The children studied Spanish and English, as well as following the Chinese curriculum, and trained at Atlético Madrid's training complex with teenagers of the same age. While they learnt to pass and head the ball, the concept of tackling another player was alien and they were uncomfortable using aggression to bustle another player off the ball. It was going to be a steep learning curve, but eventually the idea was for them to return to China and improve the standard of the new Super League.

In 2014, Wang Jianlin went to meet Miguel Ángel Gil to see how the children were getting on. It was a chance for the two men to get to know each other better and they talked courteously about business through an interpreter. Wang left Spain a few days later after buying a skyscraper in Madrid's emblematic Gran Via for €265 million – 32% less than it had cost at the height of Spain's property bubble.

A few weeks later, Gil travelled to Bengal to announce that the club had agreed to take a 25% stake in one of the franchises in a fledgling new football championship in India: Atlético Kolkata. The league's backers including Rupert Murdoch's 21st Century Fox and IMG Worldwide were keen to draw on the popularity of European football brands. Atlético would be giving its know-how but little if any cash. In return, it would plant a seed in the cricket-mad nation of 1.3 billion people that could flourish if the league took off and perhaps win it millions of new fans.

The franchises hired footballers such as David Trezeguet, Alessandro del Piero and Freddie Ljungberg. The veterans, nearing the end of their careers, were put up in luxury hotels while they trained and played in the country between September and December. With the first season barely over, Gil was back in Asia to cement a new deal with Wang Jianlin. The billionaire had seen first-hand how the Chinese teenagers were improving. They passed the ball crisply in

the Spanish style mastered by Iniesta and Xavi, known as "tiki-taka",
and while there was not a superstar like Messi amongst them,
they clearly had talent. Some had even learnt a dark art from their
Spanish peers: how to dive to win a penalty. Now Wang wanted to
increase the number of Chinese youngsters coached by Atlético's
youth-team coaches to 144 within two years. In return, the Dalian
Wanda Group he led would pay €45 million to take a 20% stake in
Atlético from Gil and co-owner Cerezo. One of Wang's executives,
Zhang Lin, joined Atlético's board. The Chinese billionaire also
agreed to invest another €15 million in the sports facility where
the youngsters trained. It would become known as the Wanda
Atlético Madrid training centre.

In one of Dalian Wanda's hotels in Beijing, Gil had a pink orchid
placed into a jacket lapel by one of the hostesses at the signing event to
mark the first foreign shareholder in Atlético Madrid. For Gil, whose
stake was reduced to 52%, the cash injection was another step away
from the dark days of the financial crisis and he was rewarded when he
and the board awarded him a boost in annual salary to €650,000.

On the sidelines of the ceremony, after taking off the orchid, he
patted himself on the back. In the space of a couple of years he had
gone from scrabbling for cash to sealing a deal with one of the world's
richest men. Sounding a bit like someone who has successfully quit
smoking, he said he had weaned Atlético off doing transfer-right deals
with investment funds. The Club now had resources of its own, not to
mention a big cheque from UEFA for reaching the Champions
League final. "We have seized the opportunity that the financial
crisis brought," Gil said.

Back in Europe, clubs in Portugal and the Netherlands were
among those having more difficulty navigating past the turmoil of the
credit crunch.

Chapter 12

Working on
a Dream

J orge Mendes is reclining on a sofa in the lounge of the Hotel Villa Magna in Madrid's central boulevard, Paseo de la Castellana, next to two mobile phones and the type of Louis Vuitton wash bag some of the players he represents carry around. He is wearing a dark-blue suit and tie. He smells of aftershave and has applied pomade to his dark hair. After chatting with an acquaintance, he stands up and beckons a white-haired 60-year-old man on the other side of the lounge to come over. The older man, who is wearing a green tweed jacket, walks over and asks Mendes what he would like. It's Luís Godinho Lopes, the president of Sporting Clube de Portugal.

Sporting is part of football's aristocracy in Portugal. Lisbon is largely split between Benfica and Sporting, the reds and the green-and-whites. The team Godinho Lopes now presides over had collected 18 domestic league titles over the last 80 years and had never been relegated from the first division. In the Madrid hotel, all Mendes needs from him is confirmation of an anecdote from when Ronaldo was a teenager at Sporting; Godinho Lopes then returns to the other side of the grand lounge to resume his conversation with a female Asian company executive. He is trying to secure a stadium naming-rights sponsor to ease the club's perilous finances. That it is he who comes over to Mendes is indicative of which of the two men is most powerful.

163

Mendes's ability to broker deals between the best players and the richest clubs, plus his sideline in the transfer-rights business that began with a bet on the teenage Diego Costa, meant that he had become extremely wealthy. Between 2008 and 2014, Mendes distributed €45.3 million in dividends to himself, Sandra (who he married in 2015) and nephew Luis Correia, who organizes endorsement deals for his clients. The dividends came via Dublin-based Gestifute International. Gestifute, which followed companies like Google to Ireland for tax reasons, paid a 12.5% tax rate there, half what it would have paid in Portugal, saving Mendes more than €5 million.

In contrast, Sporting had racked up losses in 13 of the 14 previous seasons, and was more than €375 million in the red. To raise money, Lopes had sold stakes in the transfer rights in all but one of the club's 70 senior and junior squads to Mendes's Gestifute, the CAA fund managed by Peter Kenyon and Leiston Holdings, an investment vehicle managed by Pini Zahavi. Godinho Lopes had effectively pawned all the family jewels and there was nothing left to raise money. The situation was so desperate that the club couldn't even afford to pay its latest €500,000 electricity bill and was three months late with player wages. While Atlético Madrid leveraged credit from some of the same hedge funds to take the club to the Spanish league title and Champions League final, Sporting's performances were worsening. It finished seventh in the domestic league in 2013, its worst showing in its 107-year history. A few weeks after his chat with Mendes in Madrid, Godinho Lopes gave up on his quest to turn the club around. He stood down from his post. Bruno Carvalho, a genial and chubby 42-year-old, was elected by Sporting's members to replace him. He immediately entered negotiations with Sporting's bankers, Banco Espírito Santo and Banco Millennium, to restructure the team's crippling debt.

Sometimes he worked through the night with his staff to draw up a business plan that the banks would accept. The banks were sympathetic to Sporting but Portugal was in the second year of a bailout repayment programme and its financial institutions were being examined closely by the European Union, the European Central Bank and the International Monetary Fund, the triumvirate known as the Troika. Carvalho was called in to see Ricardo Espírito Santo, the reclusive 70-year-old president of Banco Espírito Santo. In a meeting at the billionaire banker's office in Lisbon's tree-lined main thoroughfare Avenida Liberdade, he told Carvalho that they both urgently needed to find a solution. "The Portuguese banks said to us nobody in Portugal would let Sporting die – it has a family of 3 million supporters – but the Troika can kill all of us," Carvalho said. Carvalho knew that he would have to lay off dozens of staff.

The wealthy banker could hardly criticize the way Sporting had sold off stakes in player transfer rights. His bank had earned €400,000 in management fees by setting up a fund allowing Lisbon-based Benfica to do the same as Sporting. The fund had acquired the rights of 12 Benfica players, including Brazilian defender David Luiz, with investors' money. Among the investors was billionaire José Manuel "Joe" Rodrigues Berardo, a colourful character who had made his fortune in gold and diamond mining in South Africa and then enlarged it in the stock market. Berardo had acquired one of the world's most expensive private art collections, with works by Pablo Picasso and Andy Warhol. He decided to put €1 million into the fund of Benfica, the club he supported and had once tried to buy.

On a spring day in 2013, Sporting president Carvalho accepted an invitation to have lunch with one of the investment funds his predecessor had worked with. He met Nelio Lucas at the Solar dos Nunes restaurant in Lisbon's Rua dos Lusiadas. The traditional wooden-beamed eatery has blue-and-white porcelain tiles on the wall below framed newspaper cuttings about famous visitors. For both men, it was a chance to get to know each other.

Lucas looked like a younger version of his compatriot Jorge Mendes: white teeth, slick black hair and immaculate clothing. In fact, he was the protégé of Pini Zahavi. He had worked for eight years for the Israeli's Soccer Investments and Representations (S.I.R.), which bought transfer rights for a group of wealthy Eastern Europeans. Lucas would run errands for Zahavi, who was in his 60s. "I owe a lot to him," Lucas said. In 2004, Zahavi had arranged for Lucas to help his friend Jonathan Barnett, the London-based player agent, take control of marketing and transfers at Portuguese club Beira-Mar. It was an unsuccessful venture that ended after one season with relegation to the second division, but Lucas gained a reputation as bright and hard-working.

Still in his early 30s, Lucas had decided to strike out on his own. Instead of operating ad hoc out of five-star hotel lobbies like Zahavi, he planned to have his own office and an aggressive business plan to invest the money of some of the Israeli's circle of acquaintances. He soon found a major client: the family of Tevfik Arif, a Kazakh property developer.

Arif, a former Soviet Union economist, had built a chain of hotels in Kazakhstan and Turkey after the collapse of Communism and, went on to develop the 46-storey Trump Soho hotel and condominium in Manhattan after securing a licensing agreement with American magnate and now US President, Donald Trump. Trump's name and contacts had "been very helpful to us in opening some doors," Arif said in 2007, when the building was launched. Trump attended the launch with his daughter Ivanka.

Another of Arif's associates was Fettah Tamince, the chief executive of the luxury Rixos hotel chain who was a powerful and well-connected businessman in his native Turkey, with assets in the British Virgin Islands. Rixos had hotels from the Swiss ski resort of Davos, where business leaders hobnobbed every January, to the Egyptian beach holiday strip of Sharm El-Sheikh.

Arif had settled in New York, buying a pad in Port Washington, an exclusive enclave on Long Island sprinkled with yacht marinas and golf clubs, near where F. Scott Fitzgerald's *The Great Gatsby* is set. He sent his son, Arif Arif, to an American university and then to head up a family office in London.

The Arifs called the enterprise Doyen Capital and hired traders to buy and sell commodities including uranium and oil. Lucas was appointed as chief executive officer of a sister company, Doyen Sports.

Flashing a welcoming smile as they met for the first time at the Lisbon restaurant, Lucas told Carvalho how he was looking forward to deepening the relationship with Sporting and could help put the team back in the virtuous circle of winning titles and generating cash from prize money, sponsorship and ticket sales. At first the Portuguese club's new president did not give his lunch meeting with Lucas much thought, but over the coming months he would keep coming back to it.

Lucas's job was to acquire the transfer rights from clubs in Spain and Portugal, like Sporting, who were being refused credit by banks. He was given a vast expenses account that allowed him the use of a private jet. He also moved into an £18 million mansion in a gated road in London's Hampstead district. The property had a three-car garage and indoor swimming pool.

Lucas had a friendly manner that disguised a sharp eye for detail and a quick temper. As a public speaker, he was excellent: eloquent and comfortable speaking in English, Portuguese and Spanish. He charmed football club owners with his manner and promise of easy credit, which he said was bankrolled by wealthy investors and backed by some of the world's biggest financial institutions. The sum of $100 million for the Doyen investors was "a little drop in the ocean", he said.

Lucas, a one-time modelling agency scout, enjoyed mixing with football people in the VIP boxes of the world's most famous football stadiums, even if it meant long spells away from his young family. He regularly updated his WhatsApp profile picture with him standing alongside Pelé and other football royalty. His status, however, remained unchanged: "Always Available for a Good Deal!" For French daily *Libération* he posed for a picture standing astride the roof of Doyen's Mayfair office in a navy suit, sporting designer stubble and looking moody, with the London skyline at night behind him.

As Lucas was travelling back and forth from London to southern Europe, racking up €80 million of deals, Bruno Carvalho was still trying to restructure Sporting's debt with the Portuguese banks. The more he and bank executives sought a way forward in negotiations over the club's debt, the more they kept encountering roadblocks over the deals with the investment funds. The contracts were all lopsided in favour of the funds, triggering payouts to investors at regular intervals, according to Carvalho. "If we went left we would have to pay 10 million euros, and if we went right we would have to pay 20 million euros," he said. Doyen always came out a winner, in fact, in its deals with clubs. It negotiated to, at the very least, get its money back plus interest of 10% per year. That was a satisfying return on investment for Doyen's wealthy investors at a time when most banks were offering less than 1% interest to their clients.

Carvalho invited Lucas, executive Peter Kenyon and Pini Zahavi on separate occasions to his offices to discuss his problem, and try to find a solution with the investment funds they represented. All three appeared sympathetic and said they would go back to their board of directors for guidance. But, according to Carvalho, they did nothing. "The time was running out, I had to finish the restructuring," Carvalho said. "They said they would help but nothing was happening. It was like a horror movie. We were alone."

Carvalho's mind kept returning to his lunch date with Lucas. "What I saw in the agreements was something that only defended one side: the funds," Carvalho said. "The funds were saying: I will give you money that will make you stronger and stronger but in reality it was killing the club." In one deal, Doyen had acquired 75% of the transfer rights of defender Marcos Rojo for €3 million, but the contract stipulated that Doyen must receive at least €4.2 million in return over the course of his five-year contract. If another club offered €8 million for Rojo and Sporting didn't want to trade him, Doyen Sports could claim up to €6 million.

Carvalho said he wanted to retain the Argentine player because he was a key member of the squad but, according to a statement published on the club website, Lucas sent him a text message one day saying the defender would "make trouble" if he wasn't transferred. Lucas, in a phone interview, denied that he made such a threat. On 5 August 2014, according to Carvalho's version of events, Lucas turned up unannounced at Sporting's stadium with Southampton football club executive director Les Reed, Rojo's agent Carlos Gonçalves and lawyer Gustavo Galasso.

With many of Sporting's directors out of town on holiday amid sweltering heat in Lisbon, it fell to the youngest board member Alexandre Godinho to welcome them into an air-conditioned meeting room for talks about signing Rojo before the transfer window closed a few weeks later. Lucas did not introduce himself to the young director as working for Doyen, and spoke only in English, Carvalho said in a phone interview with the authors. Lucas "never pretended to be someone else", according to Doyen's court submission. Godinho reported back on the meeting to the rest of the board. Following the talks, Southampton offered €17 million to sign Rojo.

However, three days later, Manchester United's executive vice-chairman Ed Woodward lodged a higher bid of €20 million by email, copying in Lucas on the message. On paper, that fee would give the hedge fund Lucas represented €15 million, a 400% return on its investment two years earlier, and Sporting €5 million. Carvalho felt that the club with a yellow lion on its green crest was losing out. "If you are fearful, you act like a sheep, you are not a leader," Carvalho said.

Carvalho sent a letter on headed Sporting paper by courier DHL to Doyen saying that the club was rescinding all its agreements with Doyen, citing the influence Lucas had on Rojo's transfer as violating the terms. "It was Doyen who was promoting and forcing this transfer, violating his (sic) duty to respect Sporting's independence in transfer related matters," Carvalho wrote. He refused to pay Doyen Sports its €15 million share of the deal.

Ruling on the dispute, the Court of Arbitration for Sport dismissed Carvalho's complaint and ordered Sporting to pay up. It found that the club had "willingly and consciously" agreed to sell 75% of Rojo's rights to Doyen and even sought the hedge fund's help to secure a transfer for the Argentine player and other squad members.

Aside from Sporting, another top-line European team had been caught short by the financial crisis and was pulled into a scandal that involved Doyen. FC Twente, based in the Dutch town of Enschede, where Grolsch beer is made, had caused a stir by winning the 2010 Dutch championship. The success came on the back of a cash injection from local businessmen Joop Munsterman, who had worked his way up from menial jobs to become chief executive of a local newspaper group and had turned his attention to the small club near the border with Germany. He hired former England coach Steve McLaren and spent more money than usual on player recruitment.

Munsterman, who was in his 50s, liked to play his guitar after getting up in the morning and one of his favourite tunes was Bruce Springsteen's *Working on a Dream*. The song he strummed while sitting on his bed became the theme tune of Twente's title push against the decades-long dominance of Ajax Amsterdam, PSV Eindhoven and Feyenoord.

> Now the cards I've drawn's a rough hand, darling
> I straighten the pack and I'm working on a dream.

He finished a speech to fans with the last phrase of the chorus line and on the penultimate day of the season, against 14-time champion Feyenoord, the stadium resounded with the words of the song. The next week, Twente won the first league championship in its 45-year history. Munsterman, who had recorded the fans singing the Springsteen tune, sent a tape to the American singer who sent him a note back saying: "Sometimes dreams come true."

Munsterman doubled the size of the club's stadium to 24,000 seats, adding 50 sky boxes and a restaurant, and attracted fresh investment from Aldo van Laan, the heir to a tinned-meat company, who had ploughed more than €10 million of his fortune into the club. But then the financial crisis hit, and when Twente failed to qualify for the UEFA Champions League, VIP ticket sales in the sky boxes that had been worth millions for games against Milan's Internazionale and Tottenham Hotspur dried up. Twente could not keep up with payments to finance the refurbishment of the snazzy stadium. Banks shut down their credit lines to the club.

Munsterman and Van Laan turned to Doyen for a lifeline. "We had no-one else we could go to," Van Laan said. "The banks would not help us anymore." The club sold stakes in the rights of seven players to Doyen Sports in exchange for €5 million in cash. The agreements were revised and approved by the Koninklijke Nederlandse Voetbalbond (KNVB), the Dutch football federation, which did not have any rules preventing such deals.

The Netherlands, like the UK, was a conduit for agents or investors to route profits from transfer-rights deals because of tax-efficient company laws. When Atlético Madrid signed Radamel Falcão from Porto in 2011, almost €1.8 million of the fee was sent to the bewilderingly named Natland Financieringsmaatschappij B.V., which did not have to disclose its shareholders under Dutch law. Its parent company was affiliated with Broward Capital Inc. in the British

Virgin Islands. The percentage the investors paid to the Dutch treasury was less than €180,000 before the money was routed offshore.

In another transaction that year, Italian club AS Roma paid Amsterdam-based company Orel B.V. €1.6 million as part of Erik Lamela's transfer from River Plate and furnished Martijn Odems, who works at the same address in the Dutch city, with a further €3.2 million according to a financial statement by Roma. Odems, who had become a player agent six weeks before according to FIFA's public records, declined to comment – not that he was obliged to – on why he and Orel had shared in 40% of Lamela's transfer fee, when we contacted him by phone to ask for more details.

While such operations were within the rules, Van Laan had made one infraction: crucially, he had not disclosed some of the details of the transfer-rights agreements with Doyen to the KNVB. In November 2015, the terms of one deal were posted on a mysterious website called Football Leaks that had started to flood the Internet with contracts involving Doyen and football clubs that appeared to have been hacked from the Internet server of its legal advisor. The website gained even more attention when it leaked the contract between Real Madrid and Tottenham in the 2013 transfer of Gareth Bale. The deal showed that the transfer fee was €100 million, significantly more than what Real had told journalists it was.

For transfer compliance officials, the Football Leaks website was a useful tool according to FIFA's Mark Goddard, who said it showed the "wheeling and dealing" in the market. The Dutch federation was intrigued by the new information it had received about the agreement between Doyen and Twente. "The contract published seems to differ from what we know," KNVB spokesman Hans van Kastel told the Reuters news agency. While the KNVB did not immediately specify what the violation was, it appeared that Twente had allowed Doyen too much control over transfer decisions. Van der Laan quit as president as the investigation got underway. Munsterman, the guitar-strumming Bruce Springsteen fan, had bailed out of the stricken club earlier in the year.

Although the football authorities in Portugal and Spain had a long history of being lenient with clubs over their finances, the KNVB has a reputation for being unforgiving. The Dutch federation had some of the strictest licensing rules in world football. That was perhaps part of the Dutch Calvinistic heritage that today co-exists with the marijuana cafes and brothels of liberal Amsterdam – and the low-tax companies that distribute dividends offshore.

The Dutch are cautious with their money, shunning purchases on credit. Some 97% of payments in the Netherlands are with debit cards. In the same way, Amsterdam-based Ajax, which won the last of its four European Cups in 1995, had spurned transfer market speculation, even as it fell behind richer Spanish and Premier League teams in the continental pecking order.

In 2015, Premier League chief executive Richard Scudamore noted that its smallest club Burnley now earned more than Ajax, because of the English championship's booming television deals. As Burnley took out high-interest loans to sign players, Ajax continued to work within its means, hoarding more than €100 million in the bank and relying on youth-team recruits to bolster its first team. According to a 2014 report by S&P Capital IQ, Ajax had the best credit rating in a survey of 44 leading teams, just ahead of Arsenal.

FC Twente's strategy of speculating on the transfer market cast it as the black sheep of Dutch football. So it looked like the club was heading for some bad news, and so it proved. After ruling that it had "deliberately misled" the KNVB's licensing committee, Twente was banned from the Champions League and Europa League until 2019, and, according to a federation executive, its very existence was now hanging by a thread.

The KNVB stopped short of stripping Twente of its licence, instead relegating it to the second division for the 2016–17 season.

With substantially less television revenue at that level, Twente's hopes of meeting its debt payments and surviving were still slim. But there was a final twist. Twente filed an appeal, and a few days before the verdict was due raised the stakes by declaring it would have to file for bankruptcy if relegated. It was the strongest card team executives could play. Fearing it would be responsible for pushing the club out of business, the Dutch federation finally broke with its hardline approach at the last moment and let Twente stay on in the top division.

Chapter 13

The Baur
au Lac

Finally, after 10 months of exhaustive research, the report FIFA had commissioned on the involvement of funds in the transfer market landed on the desk of president Sepp Blatter. The 136-page report, signed off by six authors, found that almost 10% of global transfer fees were now distributed to investors. The report did not make a specific recommendation on whether to ban the practice, but made it clear that football had to do something urgently because the practice was becoming difficult to control. The hands-off approach FIFA had adopted wouldn't be feasible anymore.

The following month, FIFA held its annual congress in São Paulo on the eve of the 2014 World Cup. Coverage of the event was dominated by Blatter's suggestion that he would be standing for a fifth term, even though he'd promised delegates when he was re-elected in 2011 that he wouldn't. Few in the conference room paid as much attention when the soft-spoken Englishman Geoff Thompson, a former FIFA vice-president, provided an update on what was called third-party ownership of transfer rights. Thompson, sometimes unflatteringly referred to as "Silent Geoff" in the British media, said that FIFA would set up an advisory panel that might lead to new global regulations. Given the influence of South Americans in FIFA's all-powerful executive committee, few at that point could

have considered the possibility of an outright ban. Indeed, FIFA legal
director Marco Villiger was briefing reporters that a cap on the
number of players clubs could sell the transfer rights to was more
likely than prohibition.

The 68-year-old Thompson, who lived in a modest suburban
home in the northern English town of Chesterfield, would lead the
20-man panel on behalf of FIFA. The other members were representatives of national leagues, clubs and player unions. The panellists
in favour of banning investment funds included Arsenal CEO Ivan
Gazidis and Theo van Seggelen, general secretary of international
players union FIFPro. Those who wanted to regulate the arrangements were in a vocal but noisy minority, and included Spanish
league president Javier Tebas, Costa Rican football federation
president Eduardo Li and FC Porto lawyer Daniel Lorenz. The
group converged on FIFA's $250 million headquarters with its five
underground levels and walls made of grey and black granite
imported from Brazil. They walked through the sliding doors
past a meditation room made of brown onyx that contained a single
bench and, according to FIFA staff, was barely used. On level-3, the
group of 20 men strolled into the executive committee meeting
room. It was here that FIFA's "Exco" members – like Blatter, Julio
Grondona and Michel Platini – met after sweeping into the underground car park through a tunnel without having to face the waiting
TV crews and journalists.

The invited group of what FIFA called "football stakeholders"
filled most of the 24 brown leather chairs positioned under an
enormous chandelier shaped like the bowl of a football stadium
and exchanged greetings across a stone floor made of deep-blue "lapis
lazuli." In the middle of the blue was a gold-plated stone that
contained earth from each of FIFA's 207 member federations.
With FIFA and UEFA lawyers watching from the sidelines, both
sides got down to business and presented their arguments.

At times Thompson struggled to keep order as the delegates strained to make their points clear, with translators babbling into their headsets. Speaking in Spanish, Tebas said that investors were needed to provide finance to medium-sized clubs such as Atlético Madrid. Banning funds from football would be like banning sports betting because of a few cases of fraudsters fixing match results. The only measure that football authorities needed to take was to start a register of the funds and their stakes.

Gazidis, following the line of Premier League chief Richard Scudamore, calmly but thoroughly ripped into the dangers of outside interference in the transfer market. Gazidis said that the report suggested there was evidence that the practice pushed clubs into a cycle of debt and dependency. Furthermore, it was almost impossible to regulate the practice. There was even a danger, he said, that investment funds could become more powerful than clubs and dominate the $5 billion market. He said that FIFA should ban investors and introduce heavy sanctions for clubs who continued to do deals with them.

Van Seggelen, the FIFPro president who had travelled from the organization's headquarters in Amsterdam, had an even more radical view. He wanted to see the downfall of the transfer system altogether, removing the price tags associated with players once and for all. In the opinion of FIFPro, the transfer system had become a multi-billion-euro "monster" in which players were treated as commodities. Privately, union officials were holding talks with the European Commission with a view to ending the horse trading because football authorities had shown no appetite for overhauling the system themselves. FIFPro, which had helped fund Jean-Marc Bosman's successful challenge of the transfer system 20 years earlier, now wanted a wider reform of the transfer system to give footballers the same freedom of movement as other workers and not intertwine their careers with the financial outlook of club executives and investors.

But after months of trying, Van Seggelen had made no progress in negotiations with FIFA, UEFA and leading European clubs. The big clubs said they could see no better alternative to the transfer system and relations between FIFPro and the clubs had become tense. Across the lapis lazuli, the Dutchman clashed with FC Porto's lawyer over the way the market operated.

The sometimes acrimonious meeting lasted several hours before the stakeholders went their separate ways. Even though there was no consensus, as La Liga boss Tebas caught a flight back to Madrid he thought that he had made his point and expected there would be a compromise to satisfy everyone. After all, Gazidis said, he did not want clubs partnering with investors to "be thrown under a bus".

Three weeks later, a separate 24-man FIFA committee led by German football executive Theo Zwanziger that didn't include Tebas held another meeting about the issue at the ruling body's head-quarters. The group was handed a surprise last-minute mandate: they must vote that same day on whether to ban investment funds, according to one of the members, Rinaldo Martorelli, the Brazilian players' union chief, who had flown in from São Paulo. Behind the scenes, Platini and other European football officials were pushing FIFA to kick out investors. "I would have liked more time to reflect, but there was a lot of pressure from Europe to make a decision," Martorelli said. "They wanted to make a decision in one day." For the Brazilian, the issue was complex and deep-rooted in his home country, and he needed to think it over. The panel voted 22-2 in favour of a ban. Its decision would be presented to FIFA's executive committee the following day.

The next morning FIFA's 24 executives, including Platini, filed into the soundproof basement of its glass-fronted headquarters where they held meetings every few months. Three floors under-ground, they were out of range of a mobile phone signal. No longer among them was vice-president Julio Grondona, who had been

Blatter's unerring ally during his presidency. Grondona had died weeks after watching Argentina lose the World Cup final 1-0 to Germany on a heart-breaking goal deep in extra time. Blatter flew to his old friend's wake and funeral in Buenos Aires, which was attended by Argentina's president Cristina Kirchner and four-time world player of the year Lionel Messi. Standing over his dead body, Blatter shared a final moment with his old friend. "Julio, how can this be?" Blatter said, softly, as curious bystanders looked on. "You said you would always be there for us and now you have gone without telling us."

In Zurich, the FIFA executives took their usual seats with their minds made up about the issue in question. When Blatter stood up and asked if there was a consensus for a ban, the executives nodded and agreed there was. As was often the case, no vote was necessary, according to Michel d'Hooghe, a retired Belgian surgeon who had been an executive since 1988. He said executives had voted no more than five times in a quarter of a century. "The problem with voting is that you end up with the majority who are happy and the minority who are unhappy," he said.

Shortly afterwards, FIFA general secretary Jérôme Valcke briefed reporters upstairs about the decision. He said the prohibition would probably come into force in three or four years. "The ban cannot be implemented immediately," Valcke explained.

The 20 members of the working group returned to Zurich for another meeting, with the supporters of investment funds angry that their advice had been overlooked. La Liga president Tebas was particularly incensed. He felt their previous discussion had been a charade. Although there was no evidence of Platini leaning on FIFA president Blatter personally to speed up the process, there appeared to have been some bargaining between UEFA and FIFA officials. Platini had recently decided not to stand against his former running mate in the 2015 presidential election.

UEFA lawyer Alasdair Bell said there was overwhelming support for a ban in football. "The majority view was it was a practice that should be outlawed and this was a big majority view," Bell said. "It wasn't even a close call." Brendan Schwab, an Australian representing FIFPro on the working group, said he would not have been surprised if the ban was motivated by political machinations. Less than two months later, FIFA released a statement saying the prohibition would be on 1 May 2015. The six-line announcement was buried under the latest developments in an internal ethics investigation into voting on the 2018 and 2022 World Cups in Russia and Qatar. It looked like the end of the road for the 40-year-old secondary market.

Tebas decided to fight back. He was determined to defend the business model and said it was essential to provide some competitive balance as he feared the Premier League's soaring television revenue would eventually give its clubs an unfair advantage in the Champions League. Some of Spain's biggest teams – like Atlético Madrid, Valencia and Sevilla – already generated less television revenue than Premier League back-markers and the financial gulf between the two leagues continued to widen. "If we can't use this in five years' time the Premier League will be like the NBA and none of the other championships will be relevant anymore," Tebas said. His counterpart in Portugal, Luis Duque, agreed. Both men travelled to Brussels to file a complaint to the European Commission's competition department. They said that FIFA's ban would contravene rules on the free movement of capital in the European Union.

Doyen Sports, which had invested $100 million in the previous three years, filed a lawsuit against the ban to a court in Paris. The complaint said the fund would have to shut down its business within months. Platini's lieutenant Gianni Infantino said he was prepared for the backlash. "Some people see that they are going to lose money, they start hiring lawyers, they defend their position," Infantino said. "They will try to find ways around it. These guys are clever people but we are more clever." UEFA filed its own complaint to the European Commission, saying investors were undermining the integrity of the game.

■ ■ ■

Less than a month after FIFA's ban came into force, one of the members of the working group, Eduardo Li – president of the Costa Rican football federation who had opposed the ban on investment funds – returned to Zurich and checked into the Baur au Lac hotel. Li was staying on the fourth floor, his room just off the hotel's central spiral staircase. Discrete and palatial with suites costing as much as $4,000 per night, the hotel offered sweeping views of the cobalt waters of Lake Zurich and had become the resting place of choice for FIFA executives when they came to town for meetings.

While Platini was still in Warsaw for the Europa League final, other FIFA executives strolled about the hotel contentedly. Outside, black Mercedes-Benz limousines awaited them and their partners should they want to visit designer stores or swing by high-end restaurants. Some of the executives gathered in little groups, chatting over tea in the hotel's main lounge. There was a lot to discuss. In three days there would be a presidential election. Sepp Blatter was up against a Jordanian prince – Ali bin al Hussein – even if the Swiss incumbent was expected to coast to victory. One of the executives, Jeffrey Webb, a burly Cayman Islander, took his leave. With his arms draped over the shoulder of his doctor wife, Webb strolled across the hotel's marble floor and made for the grand staircase and for bed.

As the FIFA executives enjoyed themselves, excitable journalists from the *New York Times*, Bloomberg News and a few other American media organizations had gathered at the bar of the hotel. They had been tipped off that something important was going to happen. The tip-off from the US authorities a couple of days earlier was cloaked in secrecy, in case news filtered through to the FIFA men, but the reporters felt they were about to witness history. Just a few hours later, as the sun was beginning to rise, more than a dozen plainclothes police officers streamed into the hotel. Some were bearing green folders, which contained a list of names.

Webb and Li were among six people on the list. Handed key cards, the officers woke the unsuspecting FIFA officials. Two officers knocked on Li's door. He was allowed to bring a bag of belongings with a FIFA logo before they escorted him to the elevator and through a side door to a waiting car. Hotel staff held up crisp white linen to hide him and Webb from the view of the media.

The Swiss police were carrying out raids on behalf of the US Department of Justice. Led by the diminutive Loretta Lynch, a formidable lawyer who'd recently risen to the office of Attorney General of the United States, the Americans laid out a stunning array of charges, alleging that some of football's most senior men had been involved in corruption dating back more than two decades. The accused executives included elderly FIFA officials from Uruguay and Brazil who had recently attended Grondona's funeral.

Most of the charges concerned officials from the Americas who were accused of receiving millions in kickbacks in return for media and sponsorship rights, but details of suspected vote rigging in FIFA elections and bids to host the World Cup were also revealed. Blatter's name was not on the list of those people charged. FIFA's spokesman, Walter de Gregorio, made a point of saying as much when he convened an impromptu press conference. "The president is not involved," de Gregorio said. "It's not good in terms of image, in terms of reputation, but in terms of cleaning up everything we did in the last four years, this is good."

On the other side of the Atlantic, oblivious to events in Zurich, Jochen Lösch touched down at John F. Kennedy airport in New York on a flight from São Paulo. Lösch, a German sports executive, had come for a friend's wedding. As he turned off flight-mode to activate his mobile phone, he found he had received 50 WhatsApp messages from family, friends and colleagues during the 10-hour flight. Lösch, the head of international business at Traffic Sports, who had lived in Brazil for 15 years, had heard rumours in recent weeks at work that something "heavy" would happen. The company he worked for sold television rights to football tournaments, ran investment funds and owned small teams in Portugal and Brazil that aimed to profit from the player transfer market. Scanning his messages and eyeing rolling CNN updates on a TV monitor as he waited to pick up his suitcase on the baggage carousel, he quickly found out why he'd suddenly become so popular.

As part of the 236-page US indictment leading to the arrests at the Zurich hotel, it emerged that his boss, José Hawilla, had five months earlier secretly pleaded guilty in a New York court to racketeering conspiracy, wire fraud and money laundering in connection with the awarding of TV rights contracts since the 1990s. As a result of this and the evidence of other cooperating witnesses, police had charged one of Lösch's colleagues, a 44-year-old American called Aaron Davidson. Stunned by the news and a little nervous, Lösch hauled his suitcase off the conveyor belt and walked towards passport control. "I said to myself, today is D-Day," Lösch recalls.

Lösch had arrived in Rio de Janeiro to start a new unit for sports marketing agency Sportfive. Other European agencies would follow as Brazil won the rights to host the 2014 World Cup and 2016 Olympic Games. But Hawilla, the son of a dairy plant owner from São Paulo's farming belt, already dominated the market. He had turned a company that sold bus stop advertising – Traffic – into the biggest sports marketing company in Brazil. For the Brazilian football federation, he secured $1 million sponsorship deals with Pepsi and Umbro. When Nike bought out Umbro's deal and Coca-Cola gazumped Pepsi as Brazil's sponsor, Hawilla was rewarded with $2 million in annual fees over several years.

As a sideline, Hawilla also started two $20 million investment funds that bought transfer rights from clubs on behalf of investors, but he also took another direction: between 2005 and 2011 he set up or acquired three football teams – Desportivo Brasil, Estoril Praia in Portugal and Miami FC in the North American Soccer League – to make money from transfers. In 2007, Hawilla hired Lösch to oversee their management.

The beauty of owning the teams for Hawilla was that there was no interference in player trading from team executives, agents or anyone else, because Hawilla controlled the clubs and Traffic represented the players. "This is the future," Hawilla said in 2010. "There is nothing more obvious and clean than this."

Nor was there pressure from fans: the teams hardly had any. Based a three-hour drive from São Paulo, the lush green pitches on which Desportivo trained welcomed only a few dozen friends and family of players to matches. Across the Atlantic, in a suburb a 30-minute drive from Lisbon, Estoril Praia's stadium was hemmed in by apartment blocks and terraced houses and only a few hundred people turned up to watch games. Miami FC welcomed barely 1,000 fans to its games at a former high-school stadium in Fort Lauderdale.

It was a fresh approach to making money on the transfer market that, Lösch said, for investors was less troublesome and more profitable than the investment funds. But would Lösch and these clubs be hauled into the sprawling American investigation into football? Lösch held his head up and looked straight at the American immigration official examining his passport. When he was waved through to the other side, Lösch breathed a sigh of relief and the tension in his body subsided. "No-one wanted to talk to me, which proved I'm a clean guy," he said.

Chapter 14

The End Game?

In the meetings at FIFA headquarters in the weeks before the Baur au Lac raid, the Arsenal chief executive Ivan Gazidis had made a special request to the ruling body's legal chief Marco Villiger. Gazidis, an American with a friendly manner and annual compensation of £2 million, said it was "imperative" that investors and funds should not be able to buy small teams to enable them to carry on seeking profits in the transfer market. It appeared a call in vain. In England, where even third-tier clubs could attract 20,000 supporters to matches, fan pressure might help prevent this but in some parts of the world it was another matter. There was no rule in football that a club owner must chase trophies rather than financial profit.

Traffic executive Jochen Lösch freely admitted that the primary goal of the three teams they owned was financial gain. Desportivo Brasil played in the fourth tier of a regional state championship, posting clips on YouTube so that scouts of first-division clubs could track the progress of the teenagers. Despite having no fans, a framed Manchester United shirt above the reception desk and Nike swooshes adorning the two-bunk bedroom doors showed that the sports industry was watching carefully. Lösch explained to us Traffic's 2008 agreement with Manchester United. "The idea was, we scout players together, we put them in Desportivo, we share the costs and then we see how they develop," Lösch said. "It makes no sense to bring the players to England at 14. It's illegal and stupid."

Traffic spent about $4 million a year on the education and welfare of hand-picked teenagers ranging in age from 14 to 18. United could sign the players after their 18th birthday for fees already written into contracts with Traffic, Lösch said. For Traffic it was a way to make money. For United it was a means to bypass sky-high transfer fees and hefty payments to intermediaries.

Desportivo began winning regularly in Brazil, defeating the youth team of Santos, which had nurtured Pelé and Neymar. Sporting braces on their teeth, cheeky smiles and fluorescent yellow and orange Nike boots, Desportivo Brasil's Under-16 team swept to the Milk Cup title in Ballymena, Northern Ireland in 2012. Cutting through defences with slick passing, they downed Benfica 6-0 and finished off Newcastle United 3-0 in the final. After collecting the trophy, the Brazilian teenagers took a few slurps of milk from the silver cup and doused each other with the rest.

But the transition from teen prodigies to adult stars was more difficult. Lösch had experienced this with Traffic's investment funds that bought the transfer rights of teenage Brazilians. About 80% of them didn't make it. Finding the next Neymar in a country of more than 200 million people was not easy. "The player just turns out to be not as good as you had thought," Lösch said.

Desportivo left-back Rafael Leão was loaned to United in late 2011 and striker Bruno Gomes met Alex Ferguson two years later, but neither secured a deal with Manchester United. Another Desportivo player, Guilherme Delatorre, had a four-month loan stint at Queens Park Rangers in 2014 but did not feature in a single game.

To help make the transition to European football easier for the young Brazilian players, Hawilla bought Portugal's Estoril Praia in 2009 for €200,000 when it was in the second division. Hawilla sent over a dozen players from Desportivo Brasil, housing them in a slightly shabby whitewashed apartment block across the road from the club's stadium. Although the Brazilians took time to acclimatize, in the second season they helped Estoril Praia win the second-division championship title and follow up with fifth place in the first division in 2013. Hawilla's team even finished the season ahead of Lisbon-based Sporting.

That finish was enough to qualify for the UEFA Europa League for the first time in the club's 74-year history. However, sticking to its business model, it traded seven of the club's best players, including defender Ismaily Gonçalves dos Santos, who went to Shakhtar Donetsk for a €5 million fee.

On a September evening in 2013, Estoril Praia made its Europa League debut at its 5,000-seat stadium against two-time champion Sevilla. One of the two stands was filled with Spanish fans waving flags and singing noisily. For the few hundred locals in the opposite stand, this was an unprecented occasion. Sebastião "Seba" de Freitas Couto Jr., a 21-year-old striker, one of six Brazilians in the squad, crossed himself as he came out onto the field. With the match on television, this was a chance to make a name for himself and join a bigger club. Although Sevilla won 3-2 over two matches, Seba and his teammates were impressive against the team that would go on to win the tournament. Traffic's Portuguese team finished the season with a healthy €1.6 million profit and before long Seba would be traded to Olympiacos in Greece for a fee of €1.8 million.

It was the latest hit in the sprawling business empire of Hawilla. In the summer of 2014, he owned 19 companies with interests in shopping centres, golf courses and farming equipment, as well as football clubs on three continents. The revenue from around the world flowed offshore into Hawilla's British Virgin Islands-based company Continental Sports Marketing. In an article entitled "The Owner of Our Football," a reporter from O Globo interviewed Hawilla about his successful 30-year career. When asked about rumours of cronyism and corruption in his football television rights business, he was imperious. "It's just half a dozen sports reporters" making those claims, he said. "It's more jealousy and dislike than anything because in the end they want a more professional game like us. Even if you work honestly, with transparency and dignity, as we've always done here, people gossip."

Having managed to protect his reputation and enormous wealth by fending off rumour-mongers in this way for years, the FBI investigation had blindsided Hawilla, blowing a hole in his life's work. When Lösch visited the 72-year-old Brazilian in New York in 2015, Hawilla was a cooperating witness for the FBI and looked frail after cancer treatment. The Americans had required Hawilla to wear a wiretap during a meeting in Miami to try and implicate his colleagues when bribes were allegedly agreed upon for the 2015 Copa Ameria tournament in Chile.

One of them, Traffic executive Aaron Davidson, initially pleaded not guilty and was released on a $5 million bond by a court in New York. Out of nowhere, the investigation was a "Black Swan" moment for Hawilla. "Everyone hates him now and it's tough," Lösch said.

As part of his plea bargain, Hawilla agreed to pay $151 million to the US authorities and to raise money was selling off his football clubs. He sold Fort Lauderdale Strikers to investors including former Brazil striker Ronaldo and Desportivo Brasil to Chinese Super League team Shandong Luneng for about $10 million. Manchester City, the then Premier League champion, began talks about acquiring Estoril Praia. City planned to use the team, which Lösch also valued at roughly $10 million, to develop players for its squad, but its interest came to nothing.

Just as Hawilla was selling his teams that had started to do well from the transfer market, there were signs his model was catching on elsewhere. On a cold day in December 2015, an Oxford University professor in his late 40s left his apartment in an elegant townhouse in the city and made his way past historic colleges and students on his way to a meeting in a hardscrabble town in Belgium.

The small border town of Mouscron is a 20-minute taxi ride from the train terminal in the French city of Lille, which in turn is a one-hour ride on the high-speed Eurostar from London. As you travel by car across the border, the landscape is dominated by humble terraced housing, litter-strewn roads and virtually no official indication that you are crossing from France into Belgium.

A few metres inside the town limits of Mouscron there are flashing neon lights attached to a cluster of shops on the same street. The signs say "Tabac Magic," "Tabac Luxe" or "Tabac du Monde," hawking their only ware: tobacco. Cigarettes in Belgium are cheaper than in France, and the town of 57,000 has 64 tobacconists – more than one for every thousand people. They lure French retailers and smokers looking for a bargain. A packet of Marlboro reds typically costs €6 in these Mouscron shops, €1 less than in France. Not a huge saving, but if you buy a couple of tubs of 620 cigarettes, the trek to this unremarkable town is worthwhile. Belgian police sporadically raid these tobacco shops, pulling them up for illegally staying open after 8 p.m., and locals complain about the noisy clientele.

The Oxford University professor's taxi zips past these shops and arrives at his destination: Le Canonniere, the glass-fronted stadium of Royal Mouscron, the smallest team in the Belgian first division. (The club, 500 m from the French border, has an average crowd of some 4,000 fans at home games in the 11,300-seat arena.)

Gil Zahavi, who teaches modern Hebrew at Oxford University's faculty of Oriental Studies, is the son of Israeli dealmaker Pini Zahavi. Zahavi Sr., the ally of transfer market investors for two decades, had led a takeover of the club a few months earlier for €2.5 million, just as FIFA was banning his main business. The acquisition was through a company called Gol Football Malta Ltd. Pini Zahavi put his son Gil and nephew Adair on the board of the club, and they arrive for a 10 a.m. board meeting on this December day, to be greeted by the club's president Edward van Daele and a few French directors.

Zahavi's son did not have any equity in the business, although his nephew did have a stake. Neither received any renumeration from the club. Pini Zahavi did not attend the board meeting himself, although he had turned up for a game a few weeks earlier, wrapped in a scarf and overcoat, with a cap pulled down over his forehead.

The 72-year-old Israeli, does not want to speak about why he has acquired this modest club, which has repeatedly struggled to avoid bankruptcy in recent years. He would only tell French newspaper *L'Equipe* that "we need time, we are in the middle of changing things". According to Van Daele, Zahavi was attracted to the country by "interesting" financial rules. Under Belgian tax law, 95% of the club's dividends are tax deductible after one year because of the €2.5 million invested.

After signing off on a loss – for accounting reasons, according to the club's financial statement – for the previous year, Gil Zahavi and the other directors discuss mundane matters like hiring an extra groundsman and organizing language lessons for the multi-national squad. Since Zahavi's acquisition, Mouscron has signed 30 players, including seven in the hours before the 31 August 2015 transfer deadline. 70% of the squad are from outside Belgium. They come from Turkey, France, Portugal, the Czech Republic, Romania, Slovenia, Cameroon, Argentina, Israel, the United States and Brazil.

While Pini Zahavi would not discuss his interest in the club, it appears that he will use his contacts and knowledge of the transfer market to bring success and profit. Royal Mouscron's president, Van Daele, has won a pledge that the 93-year-old club's identity will not be damaged. The days of a local businessman ploughing in money have long gone, he told *L'Equipe*. "We did not have any offer from a captain of industry or financial institution saying we'll come and save you," Van Daele, told the historic French sports daily that was started after the Second World War. "This is the reality of today. You can feel nostalgic about the football of your father's generation but you have to accept that it's over."

The board meeting lasts a little over two hours before Gil Zahavi is free to leave this humdrum working-class town with its 64 tobacco shops and return to the spires and cobbled streets of Oxford.

As FIFA's ban on investors from the transfer market came into force, another veteran dealmaker made his next move. Juan Figer, the one-time chess champion, saw the so-called bridge transfers he pioneered in the 1990s increasingly under scrutiny in South America.

Uruguay's goverment lifted the tax rate on transfer profits to as much as 30% from 3% (although owning a club meant there were ways of reducing this). In 2016, a year after its chief José Maria Marin was arrested and extradited to the USA on allegations he was involved in the FIFA corruption case, the Brazilian football federation intro-duced a rule that banned transfers with "no sporting reason".

In Argentina, the federal tax agency said it would take the unprecedented step of regulating the transfer market itself. From May 2016, all clubs had to declare transfer details to the tax agency which – taking a leaf out of FIFA's book – set up its own electronic database for teams to log information. New national legislation even gave the agency the power to estimate the transfer market price of each player and penalize clubs if it thought they were avoiding the 17.5% tax on player transfer fees.

Amid this changing landscape, Figer quietly took a 75% stake in Portimonense, a second-division team in Portugal using For Gool Co., the company which still did not list its shareholders even after the UK had changed its rules on company transparency. It was not the only one: according to *Private Eye* magazine, by the summer of 2016, more than 7,000 UK companies had not disclosed "significant" shareholders as required. The magazine likened the transparency project to a "chocolate teapot".

So For Gool, based in the English town of Rochdale, next to buildings with bricked-up windows, now controlled a club on the Algarve coast. Like Estoril Praia further north of the country, and Royal Mouscron in Belgium, it was neither a big club, nor a succesful one. Portimonense had an average attendance of 3,800 supporters and had never won a trophy in its 100-year history.

In July 2015, the €2.8 million transfer of midfielder Danilo Pereira to FC Porto was routed via Portimonense, even though he did not play a game for the second-division club. Pereira had played the previous two seasons for Maritimo on the island of Madeira. Figer signed another up-and-coming star to Portimonense in January 2016 – Nigerian striker Musa Yahaya – three weeks after his 18th birthday. The teenager had been training with Tottenham Hotspur's youth team.

Like his peers, Nelio Lucas was also pursuing a new line of business. The Doyen Sports chief executive signed an agreement with struggling Belgian club Seraing under which the company would pay €300,000 to the second-division team in return for helping to acquire two players per season. When the players were traded, Doyen would receive 30% of the transfer fees. The plan went off course when the Belgian football federation blocked one of the transfers, accusing Seraing of breaching the new FIFA ban. The world ruling body followed up by fining the club 150,000 Swiss francs and banned it from signing players for two years. It was a sign that FIFA would enforce its new regulations, but this game of cat-and-mouse would soon be overseen by a new executive.

Just after lunch one afternoon in late July 2016, the FIFA transfer market chief Mark Goddard pinged a carefully worded email to dozens of his fellow staff. With no major FIFA-organized football tournament over the summer, many were on holiday and the office in Zurich was pretty much deserted; he received several out-of-office responses. The subject line said: "Goodbye All."

The Australian was leaving the frontline of transfer market compliance after nine years and said he was looking for a new career challenge. Goddard wrote that he and his staff had made a "profound" difference to the transfer market and surprised many people in the industry with the progress they had made. If FIFA's transfer-monitoring system he had set up was a football computer game, he wrote, "I would have made it all the way to the World Cup final playing as Australia".

Perhaps surprisingly, none of FIFA's executives, who were the ultimate guardians of the transfer market, were copied into the email. "The few regrets I have are the moments that I let a lack of courage stop me from driving change," Goddard wrote.

For all the increased vigilance of the market from the authorites, it seemed that FIFA would continue to have a tricky job policing the grey areas that still existed around its transfer rules. Earlier that year a report published by Harvard University said that in soccer, there was a "deeply interconnected pyramid of money and transactions, domi- nated by a small elite and characterised by vast dark spaces, institutional voids and a profound lack of data". FIFA, the report said, has banned "third party ownership of players" by investors "without an effective means to assess if and where it exists".

We went along to the Rio de Janeiro offices of Eduardo Uram to get his view. Uram, who likes to wear silk shirts despite the tropical climate, has grown wealthy from the transfer market as an agent and investor over the last two decades. One of the leading agents in Brazil, he represents 120 footballers and among his ventures owns a third- division team called Tombense in the state of Minas Gerais, where Pelé was born.

Sitting in a cream-coloured leather chair in his office in one of the tower blocks that line Avenida das Americas in the Barra de Tijuca neighbourhood, he reflected on the evolution of the transfer market since Juan Figer, the first FIFA-approved agent in Brazil, "created the idea of economic rights of a player. What Juan Figer did was," Uram said, "like bottling air and selling it".

Uram wasn't so keen to talk about his ownership of Tombense, a team based 150 miles away in a state he had no apparent connection with. "I don't want to speak about my things," he added. Later, he conceded that some of the players Tombense registers may not play for the team before they are traded to other clubs. That, he adds, also occurs at Chelsea. Roman Abramovich's club had 34 players on loan to other teams at the end of the 2015–16 season. English player union boss Gordon Taylor said the oligarch's team was "warehousing" talent it might never field.

As we chatted with Uram, Brazil was entering a recession and analysts predicted its economy could fall into its deepest trough for a quarter of a century. Exports from the port town of Santos, where first Pelé and then Neymar became famous half a century apart, had dropped off and property prices were tumbling. However, the value of the global transfer market continued to climb year on year, rising another 3% to $4.2 billon in 2015 after a spending spurt by Chinese clubs. Since 2011, the market has increased in size by a whopping 44%.

In the summer of 2016, Manchester United pushed up the transfer market inflation a notch by paying a world record €105 million fee to Juventus for Paul Pogba, breaking the mark set by Gareth Bale's move to Real Madrid. The Italian club used €90 million to sign Gonzalo Higuain from Napoli. Rob Steen, writing for *The Guardian* newspaper, was rattled by the size of the fees. "Money doesn't just talk in football," he wrote, "it never shuts up." Overall, the 20 Premier League clubs spent more than £1 billion on signing players that summer.

Uram's office is insulated from the traffic noise on the busy road below. He says that he is unfazed by Brazil's recession and the ban on investors from the transfer market. His business, after all, is driven by markets abroad. Asked about the impending gloom at home, he responds by taking out a premium Cohiba cigar from his drawer. "You ask what I think of the crisis" he says, as he lights the Cuban tobacco with a silver Zippo lighter and blows a puff of smoke nonchalantly into the air. "This is how much I don't feel the crisis."

Epilogue

iguel Ángel Gil is at 4,000 feet in a business-class seat at the front of an Airbus A340 flying over Provence in the south of France. He is wearing a dark suit, tie askew as usual, and is carrying just an overnight case with him in the overhead locker. It's 8.40 p.m., on the last weekend in May, and it's his 53rd birthday.

In Milan, at that very moment, Atlético Madrid is about to start the Champions League final against Real Madrid – the second meeting of the teams in three years at the climax of the competition. Inside the stadium, 20,000 Atléti fans fill one end of the Giuseppe Meazza stadium, better known as the San Siro, which has played host to some of football's greatest teams. Stretched from one side to the other, they hold up a huge banner reading "Your values make us believe". Even though they are outnumbered by Real Madrid supporters, it is the Atlético fans that make most of the noise. They scream "Atléti, Atléti . . .". UEFA's idea of hiring pop star

Alicia Keys to play a short set just nine minutes before the match was perhaps ill-advised.

The previous night Gil had listened to the Milan Philharmonic Orchestra perform Strauss at the city's other famous arena, the La Scala opera house. He had also dined at the theatre, which is decorated in gold brocade and red velvet, with Real Madrid president Florentino Pérez and other officials.

After the meal, Gil had slept at the smart Meliá Milano hotel, a 10-minute drive from the stadium. After a low-key lunch with fellow shareholder Enrique Cerezo to celebrate his birthday – they closed the curtains of the hotel's function room – Gil went to his room to pack his suitcase.

At 6.40 p.m., just as the players were leaving for the stadium, Cerezo and other Atlético directors posed for a group photograph on the marble staircase to mark the occasion. Gil had already gone. He had ordered one of UEFA's fleet of hired black limousines, on call for the weekend, to take him to Milan's Malpensa airport to catch Iberia flight IB3255 home to Madrid. As usual, he was too anxious to watch the game. If he felt too tense to watch Atlético play even Spanish league games, there was no way he was going to sit through the Champions League final.

At the stadium, Cerezo sat alongside Spain's King Felipe VI, one of the few Atlético fans in the Spanish establishment. Alongside them was Gianni Infantino, Michel Platini's UEFA lieutenant between 2009 and 2015, who had told his boss about transfer market investors working with Champions League clubs in the midst of the financial crisis.

Unusually, there was no sign of Platini at the San Siro. For years, as UEFA president, he had been the man who had handed over the silver Champions League trophy known as "orejones" ("big ears" in Spanish, because of its looping handles that resemble two ears). Platini would hug the players of the winning team and try to console the losers. As a former player, he could empathize with them. But now he was banned from the stadium. He had been kicked out of the sport he had been in love with since the age of seven when he played table football at the Café des Sportifs his grandfather owned in the French town of Joeuf. Two weeks earlier, the UEFA president of eight years stepped down from his post after being banned from all football activities for four years.

Platini's downfall was the latest fallout from the American investigation into FIFA. That inquiry had prompted the Swiss to launch their own probe into the not-for-profit organization that had been based in their country since the 1930s, when it moved into a 30 m^2 office in Zurich's ritzy Banhofstrasse. In May 2015, a couple of hours after FIFA executives were arrested at the Baur au Lac hotel in a dawn raid, Swiss police slipped into the organization's headquarters and seized hard drives and other documents. They had already quietly ordered Swiss banks to hand over details of FIFA financial transactions dating back years.

After poring through the data over several weeks, the investigators came across one unusual exchange involving the two most powerful men in world football. In February 2011, a few months before Platini announced he would not stand against Blatter in FIFA presidential elections, the ruling body had wired 2 million Swiss francs to a private bank account of the Frenchman. Armed with this information, the police and prosecutors returned to FIFA headquarters. With Blatter and other FIFA executives meeting underground in their usual spot, seated around the blue "lapis lazuli" floor, the Swiss state officials walked into the building to search the president's office before summoning him for questioning.

Blatter protested his innocence, saying that the single payment to Platini was made on a verbal agreement more than a decade earlier in 1999, when the former player began a three-year stint working as his advisor. At the time, Blatter said, FIFA was having financial difficulties.

It was only in 2011, by which time FIFA had more than $1 billion in cash reserves, that Platini had asked to be paid.

Under Swiss law, there was nothing illegal about the arrangement. Yet, for FIFA's head of compliance, Domenico Scala, both men had breached their fiduciary duties by not recording the sum in FIFA accounts when the agreement was made. The ruling body's ethics committee banned both men from football for eight years and, although the sentences were subsequently reduced following appeals to four years for Platini and six years for Blatter, both men were now nursing their wounds.

Platini's stand against commercialism in football was also undermined soon after when, as part of a leak of documents from the Panamanian law firm Mossack Fonseca, it emerged that he had opened an offshore company in the tax haven called Balney Enterprises Corporation in 2007, less than a year after becoming UEFA president. Platini, whose main residence was in the Swiss village of Genolier in the foothills of the Jura mountains, said he had done nothing wrong: authorities in the country knew about the company and all his tax affairs were in order.

After losing his job, Platini kicked his heels, spending time playing golf with old friends on courses outside Paris and on the French Riviera. He was trying to "disconnect" from football, but he could not stop talking about it. He kept up a jovial front – "Am I allowed to play football in my garden?" he joked – but it was difficult for him to take, and he was already plotting a way back. At the age of 80, Blatter had no such aspirations. He had returned to the Swiss village of Visp where he was brought up.

With Platini now unable to carry through with plans to stand as FIFA president, Infantino stepped in as a candidate and, after using his political experience, fluency in five languages, some generous promises (and with the help of €500,000 from UEFA to cover his travel and campaign costs), he was elected. It was a sudden and unexpected turn of events, even for the polyglot. He now sat alongside King Felipe VI as the most powerful man in football: FIFA president.

Infantino said he was saddened by Platini's ban but would cherish "the great things" they had achieved over the previous nine years, presumably including in his mental summary the "financial fair play" rules and ban on investors from the transfer market. He now planned to continue their work as the most senior official in football. His FIFA election manifesto pledged to create "fair and transparent" player trading, FIFA, he wrote, needed to take a more hands-on approach to the transfer of footballers, to "limit abuse and tackle the exploitation of the system by external parties".

Even as he sat alongside the Spanish King, lawsuits swirled around the FIFA ban of investors from the transfer market and Neymar's move to Barcelona. In the latest development a few weeks earlier, a judge at Spain's National Court had dropped charges against the former Barcelona president Sandro Rosell. A separate case brought by Brazilian investor Delcir Sonda against Rosell, Neymar and his father was still moving slowly through the Spanish courts.

Sitting back in his business-class seat, Gil could finally try to relax a little. For the next hour or so, he had no obligations to perform as Atlético chief executive, and no way of knowing what the score was in the Champions League final. There were a thousand thoughts going through his head, all the same. Could the team, his family's heirloom, finally win its first elite European title? All the stress over the debts his father had left would be forgotten with the silver trophy. Only 22 clubs had won the European Cup since 1955 and as money played a bigger role in football, it was becoming more difficult for all but the biggest teams to win.

Winning the league two years earlier had been very special, but the Champions League would top that achievement. Atlético had earned €94 million in UEFA prize money for reaching the final and quarter final the last two years, and could look forward to another handsome payday. The club had reduced its mountainous tax debt from €120 million to about €40 million – still more than enough to be shut down in another league, but a marked improvement on three years earlier – and was pushing ahead with drawn-out plans to build a new stadium. However, triggering happiness among Atlético's legion of loyal fans – including his family and friends – would be more rewarding than the financial spinoffs of becoming European champion.

Gil and thousands of supporters had suffered enough by losing in extra time two years ago. Another loss against Atlético's arch rival would be difficult to take. Just as he was deep in thought, as the Airbus A340 passed over the seaside resort of Cannes, a teenage Atlético fan with her hair in braids in the Milan stadium burst into tears. Sergio Ramos had put Real Madrid in the lead. It was Ramos who had punctured Atlético's dream two years ago in Lisbon, with a last-gasp 93rd-minute goal.

Gil was oblivious to the torment Atlético fans in the stadium were suffering when the Iberia plane touched down in darkness at Adolfo Suárez airport in Madrid at 10:22 p.m. The match was deep into the second half and Real Madrid was still leading 1-0. As the pilot taxied to the terminal, Atlético's Belgian substitute Yannick Carrasco smashed the ball into the roof of the net to level the score.

As Gil emerges into Madrid's airport and comes out into the arrivals hall, a man recognizes him and tells him the game is now in extra time. A television reporter follows him up the escalator to the car park, jabbing questions at him. "Wouldn't it be great to win the Champions League on your birthday?" asks the reporter, grinning. "Of course, it's something we have been trying to do for 113 years" Gil says, with a tight smile. "Now please leave me in peace."

He wants to be alone at the wheel of his new Range Rover, driving in the night and listening to music until the match is over. The pace of the match slows, because both teams are tired and cautious not to make a mistake. The final will be decided by penalty kicks.

Gil is already safely behind the wheel of his new car and driving along the empty highway. At homes and bars in Spain, 13 million people – more than one quarter of the country's population – are watching the penalty shootout get underway. Real Madrid scores its first three penalties and so does Atlético. It's a tie, and the final could now be decided by a single mistake.

To the horror of Atlético fans, Juan Francisco "Juanfran" Torres steps up and smashes his kick against the post. Cristiano Ronaldo needs only to convert his for Real Madrid to win the final. He plants the ball firmly into the net, rips off his shirt and races to the side of the field to celebrate with his teammates. Juanfran breaks down in tears as he holds his bony hand to his heart and mouths "I'm sorry" to thousands of Atlético supporters.

The Atlético players are stony faced and wave away acting UEFA president Ángel María Villar as he tries to put the runner-up medals around their necks. Instead, they snatch the silver discs in their hands without looking at them, as if collecting a leaflet from a street hawker. At about the same time, while still at the wheel on a ring road on the outskirts of Madrid, Gil finds out the bad news.

Bibliography

We found the following books particularly useful for background information:

- *Beastly Fury: The Strange Birth of British Football* by Richard Sanders (Bantam, 2010)
- *Broken Dreams: Vanity, Greed and the Souring of British Football* by Tom Bower (Simon & Schuster, 2003)
- *Gol di Rapina: Il Lato Oscuro del Calcio Globale* by Pippo Russo (Edizioni Clichy, 2014)
- *La Clave Mendes* by Miguel Cuesta and Jonathan Sánchez (La Esfera de Los Libros, 2015)
- *Ma Vie Comme Un Match* by Michel Platini (Editions Robert Laffont, 1987)
- *Todo Pasa* by Hernán Castillo (Aguilar, 2012)
- *Yo Soy El Diego* by Diego Maradona (Planeta, 2000).

For details about the agent Juan Figer, the exhaustive minutes of the Brazilian Senate's 2001 parliamentary inquiry were helpful. Suzanna Andrews's excellent 2009 *Vanity Fair* story "The Widow and The Oligarchs" assisted us in better understanding the lives of Boris Berezovsky and Badri Patarkatsishvili.

Acknowledgments

The book is drawn from more than a decade of working as reporters while we were living in Brazil, Spain and the U.K. Much of that time was spent covering the business of sport for Bloomberg News.

Many of our sources prefer not to be identified. The default setting for people working in the football business is not to engage with reporters. We thank those who spoke to us off-the-record for being generous with their time.

We would also like to show our appreciation to the following:

Lucía Baldomir, Raymond Beaard, Alasdair Bell, Eduardo Carlezzo, Bruno Carvalho, Daniel Cravo, Juan de Dios Crespo, José María Gay, Miguel Ángel Gil, Tim Hewitt, David Leloup, Augusto Lendoiro, Jochen Lösch, Wil van Megen, Marcos Motta, Andrew Orsatti, Ray Ranson, Ariel Reck, Gregor Reiter, Brendan Schwab, Richard Scudamore and Javier Tebas.

On a personal note, Alex would like to thank all the Duff, Santana and Hewitt clans for their help in one way or another and especially his wife Silvia and daughters Madalena and Carlota.

Tariq would like to thank the friends and family whose support was invaluable during the years leading up to this book.

About the Authors

Alex Duff worked as a freelance reporter in Rio de Janeiro for English newspapers and Associated Press from 1998 to 2000. As a staff journalist in London and Madrid for Bloomberg News he covered the business of sport for 15 years with a special focus on European football, Formula One and the Tour de France. He now lives in the Netherlands and works for FIFPro, the world football players union.

Tariq Panja has worked as a reporter for the *Manchester Evening News*, Associated Press and Bloomberg News in London and Rio de Janeiro. He has broken news on some of the biggest stories in soccer including the takeover of Liverpool, Manchester United's float on the New York Stock Exchange and the unprecedented scandal that threatened to bring down FIFA. After covering Brazil's bumpy journey towards hosting the World Cup and Summer Olympics, Tariq has returned to the U.K. and is once again based in London.

Index